GOD'S
GREAT
PROMISES

GOD'S GREAT PROMISES

**Fifty-two Bible Promises
one for each week of the year**

W. T. H. RICHARDS

ABINGDON PRESS

NASHVILLE **NEW YORK**

GOD'S GREAT PROMISES

Copyright © W. T. H. Richards 1973
British edition published 1973
by Marshall, Morgan & Scott

ISBN 0-687-15329-8

MANUFACTURED BY THE PARTHENON PRESS AT NASHVILLE,
TENNESSEE, UNITED STATES OF AMERICA

1 Precious Promises

It is through him that God's greatest and most precious promises have become available to us men. 2 Peter 1: 4 (Phillips)

What a stimulating book the Bible is! Millions have received invaluable help from this sacred volume. It meets the needs of all. This book is 'the child's delight, the young man's sure guide and the consolation of the elderly. Within its pages the sick and burdened find the solace they need, the tempted receive succour and lost souls find the message of salvation. The Bible has inspired poets with the loftiest of themes; the philosophers with the noblest of maxims; the painters with the most admirable inspiration and the musicians with the sublimest strains.'

Undoubtedly one of the most glorious features of the Bible is that it is a treasure house containing golden promises to enrich all who reach out the hand of faith to take them. We must, of course, expect opposition from the Enemy when we attempt to do this. That great man, Trapp, said on one occasion, 'When faith would lay hold of the promises, Satan rappeth her on the fingers as it were, and seeks to beat her off.' Obtaining promises is not an easy operation, but it is a worthwhile one. The Devil contests the believer on every occasion when he seeks to appropriate for himself the things that God has planned for his benefit.

God has always intended that His people should share His wealth and He has written a Book to tell us so. The Book contains the title deeds! It has been estimated that there are 7,487 promises in the Bible made by God personally. There are hundreds of promises in some of the thirty-six books that make up the Bible. Do you know that some

5

chapters contain scores of promises and, furthermore, that there are two or three promises sometimes contained in a single verse. It is no wonder that, when Adoniram Judson was asked by his Mission Board about the prospects of the work in Burma, he replied 'The future is as bright as the promises of God.'

What a comforting thought to know that 'this God is our God.' In a world torn apart by hatred, political greed, riots and war, we can go to One who has the answer to every individual need; One who is still working out His purposes in spite of the fact that 'The kings of the earth set themselves, and the rulers take counsel together, against the Lord and against His anointed. . . . (Ps. 2: 2). Make no mistake, He will triumph and He will never forsake those who put their trust in His Word.

Let us not fear what man can do, let us put ourselves always in the hands of Him who is able to perform what He has promised. Let us not for one moment doubt that He is 'able to do exceeding abundantly above all that we ask or think' (Eph. 3: 20). What may be a stimulant to our faith are the words of Salter, who wrote, 'Every promise is built on four pillars; God's justice and holiness, which will not suffer Him to deceive; His grace or goodness, which will not suffer Him to forget; His truth, which will not suffer Him to change; His power, which makes Him able to perform.'

It is the prerogative of every believer to enter the inexhaustible mine of divine wealth, to search the sacred veins, to gather up the beautiful treasures that will enrich them. There is no excuse for spiritual poverty when we are invited to come and partake freely. Our inheritance is there to be taken and enjoyed. Some promises are unique and dispensational but there are certain promises for all believers in every generation which we should embrace with gratitude to God.

Someone asked, 'What is a promise?' and the answer

was given, 'It is a declaration of God's will, wherein He signified what particular good things He will bestow and the evils He will remove.' What could be more encouraging than this? How good our God is, and as to His faithfulness along this line, among many others we have the testimony of Solomon who said in 1 Kings 8: 56, 'Blessed be the Lord, that hath given rest unto his people Israel according to all that he promised the hand of Moses his servant.' Let us rejoice in the truth that is expressed in the hymn we used to sing years ago and which is still valid today:

> For ever! for ever! Oh, not for a day!
> He keepeth His promise for ever!
> To all who believe, to all who obey,
> He keepeth His promise for ever!

2 Never Forsaken

I will never leave thee, nor forsake thee.
Hebrews 13: 5

Here we have one of the most emphatic promises in the whole Bible. None other can possibly thrill the hearts of God's people more than this priceless jewel. It has been called by someone, 'The Pilgrim's Staff'. Certainly many a weary traveller on the road of life has leaned hard upon it and found added strength for the journey.

If we look closely at this verse, we discover that, in the original, it has five negatives. It is rendered by Doddridge, 'I will not, I will not leave thee; I will never, never, never forsake thee.' What a beautiful exposition of the faithfulness of God. What a magnanimous affirmation!

This has ever been the attitude of God towards His people. He delights to be with His own and to share the fellowship with them. This promise was made in every dispensation. It was first given to Jacob in Genesis 28: 15, and to Joshua in Joshua 1: 5. David also became a recipient, 1 Kings 8: 57, and his son, Solomon, 1 Chronicles 28: 20. It was, of course, passed on to the Christian Church.

Think of it, through good times or ill, 'He is always near to bless and cheer.' All others, no matter how near and dear they are to us must, of necessity, leave us if only for a short time. The demands of life impose limitations and restrictions upon us all. But our God is not at all frustrated by these things. He is with us every step of our journey through life. He is indeed 'A friend that sticketh closer than a brother' (Pro. 18: 24).

There is no experience in life where we need be alone. 'My presence shall go with thee' holds good, not only for the mountain-top experiences of life but for valleys as well; Isaiah 43: 2 points this out: 'When thou passest through the waters, I will be with thee; and through the rivers, they shall not overflow thee: when thou walkest through the fire, thou shalt not be burned.'

We have the guarantee, in this promise, that He will keep His word that no child of His will ever be forsaken. At times, it may appear that we are – persecution, pain, bereavement, forsaken by friends; all these things tend to make us believe that the Lord has 'forgotten to be gracious' and that He has broken His word, leaving us to struggle through on our own. But we can be sure that, through it all, He is standing by watching our actions and reactions to these things. He will not suffer us to be tempted above what we are able to bear.

We must remember that trials and temptations are not evidences that He has denied us; on the contrary, they show that He is working out His purposes in us. Someone has rightly pointed out that 'temptations serve as a file to rub off the rust of self-confidence.' In other words, we will be the better for going through such tests. This is a necessary part of the divine plan for our lives. It behoves us to learn to trust Him at all times, then He will bring us to the place of assurance and understanding. The glorious realisation will dawn upon us that He has been with us all the time and we will be able to say like Jacob of old (Gen. 28: 16), 'Surely the Lord is in this place; and I knew it not.' Hiram O. Wiley had such an assurance and the hymn based on what he wrote reads:

> He leads us on by paths we do not know;
> Upwards He leads us, though our steps be slow;
> Though oft we faint and falter on the way . . .
> Yet when the clouds are gone,
> We know He leads us on.

3 Peace

Thou wilt keep him in perfect peace, whose
mind is stayed on thee: because he trusteth
in thee. Isaiah 26: 3

It is said that, for forty years, the above text was hung on
the wall of the bedroom of Mr Gladstone, former British
prime minister. They were the first words to meet the
great statesman's eyes every morning and they were one
of the sources of his calm strength. It would make for universal peace if world leaders followed his example of
trusting the Word of God instead of their own devices.

This gift of which the Bible speaks is not the peace of ap-
athy which comes by giving up the struggle of life and adopting a couldn't-care-less attitude, culminating in moral
and spiritual stagnation. Neither is it the peace of sensual-
ism, a synthetic product of carnal behaviour and living to
gratify the lower animal nature. Nor is it the peace of
false security resulting from trusting in human reasoning.

The promise here is described as 'perfect peace.' That is
the highest possible quality. In the margin it says 'peace,
peace,' a Hebrew term denoting the superlative essence of
the gift. It enabled the Psalmist to say, 'Therefore will not
we fear, though the earth be removed, and though the
mountains be carried into the midst of the sea' (Ps. 46: 2).
It is called 'the peace of God, which passeth all understanding' in Philippians 4: 7. The writer is here alluding to
the figure of a city that is beseiged by the enemy without,
yet kept secure by a strong garrison within. Similarly,
peace stands as a sentinel guarding the soul and keeping
back any evil power that may attempt to enter and rob us
of the serenity that is promised to all believers.

How wonderful it is to know that we can enjoy an inner

calm like the serene ocean depths, untroubled by the turbulent waves and angry winds above. We are 'in' the world but not 'of it' and are thus untroubled by its constant roarings and ragings. How thrilled are those in this state of blessedness; they can sing with exultant hearts, 'Oh, the peace my Saviour gives, Peace I never knew before; For my way has brighter grown, Since I learned to trust Him more.'

Herein lies the secret of how we may obtain this peace. In the text it says 'because he trusteth in thee.' Notice also the little word 'stayed'. When the mind is stayed upon God and one's whole being trusts and rests upon Him in childlike faith, a heavenly tranquility floods the heart. Furthermore, the believer is 'kept' in this state; it is not a temporary experience. The word is translated elsewhere 'constant peace'. Through all the various vicissitudes of life the trusting Christian will remain unperturbed. His fears will be allayed and he is assured that 'all things work together for good. . . .'

God made provision for us all. All we need to do is 'trust' in the real sense of the word. We will then no longer be harrassed by pernicious doubts but will be able to say with the Psalmist, 'I will both lay me down in peace, and sleep: for thou, Lord, only makest me dwell in safety.' (Ps. 4: 8.)

4 Guidance

I will instruct thee and teach thee in the way which thou shalt go: I will guide thee with mine eye. Psalm 32: 8

Every promise has a peculiar virtue in it that meets a particular need of the Christian. Although our needs are so numerous and varied, there is a promise to match the need whatever it may be. This is one of the consolations of the true believer.

The promise under review in this Psalm is repeated in many parts of the Bible. Probably in a lesser degree these words can be applied to David, the author of the Psalms, but it is obvious when studying the full import and range of the words used, that they refer to God and His concern for the welfare of His children. This particular promise affects all believers all the time. It is for pilgrims travelling to the city of God, with a guarantee of guidance, companionship and support.

The journey of life is hazardous, it lies through difficult regions, it is beset with many snares and pitfalls. From youth to old age our steps are dogged by enemies and surrounded with perils. Yet we need not fear; we can be fortified by the fact that we have One by our side who 'knoweth the way that I take' (Job 23: 10).

At first glance it seems a strange promise to make but when we begin to ponder over it a little, the meaning becomes clear. Firstly we see God as an instructor and then as a guide. It is important that we understand what is implied in the first before we can share in the benefit of the second. We must learn certain lessons and obey the instructor before we can walk securely and confidently with the guide.

Notice, 'I will instruct thee and teach thee.' It is essential that we have a teachable disposition and that we are quick to submit to His Word. If we love God we will, just as Jesus declared in John 14: 15, 'If ye love me, keep my commandments.' But observe here that God uses another method to make known His will. He 'instructs' us through His dealings with us along the road of life. Notice 'I will teach thee in THE WAY.' In other words we are to learn through adversity, set-backs and suffering. We must believe that 'the steps of a good man are ordered by the Lord' (Psalm 37: 23). Nothing is left to chance. There is no part of the Christian life which is 'full of sound and fury, signifying nothing.' There is purpose in every step, a design and plan in each incident that is 'according to His will.' To learn this lesson thoroughly is to bring us into the conscious presence of the divine guide.

Notice the second part of the promise. The RSV reads, 'I will counsel you with my eye upon you.' This means, of course, that the Lord is constantly watching over us. He never loses sight of anyone. No need, trouble or danger is hidden from Him. He will not allow any difficulty or trial to overwhelm or divert us from the true pathway. He knows the best and safest route to take and the child of God can say with conviction, 'Led by ought else I tread a devious way, O lead me on!'

The promise also implies that we are to look up to the eye which is to guide us. It is not sufficient that His eye is fixed on us. Our eye must also be fixed on God. It is not only saying in our hearts 'thou God seest me', but we must also keep in mind the words of the Psalmist, 'They looked unto him and were lightened: and their faces were not ashamed' (Ps. 34: 5). How wonderful to be able to say with the hymnwriters:

'I trust in God where ever I may be,
Upon the land or on the rolling sea,
For come what may, from day to day
My heavenly Father watches over me.'

13

5 Desires Granted

*Delight thyself also in the Lord; and he shall
give thee the desires of thine heart.*
Psalm 37: 4.

Some folk are under the impression that Christianity is
all self-denial and that life becomes morbid and unenter-
prising if one embraces the Christian faith but, of course,
the exact opposite is the case. We begin to live life to the
full only when we come God's way. In this promise we are
offered a blank cheque, so to speak, that will meet our
need along every line! This certainly needs investigating.
In the New Testament we see Jesus substantiating this
amazing promise in John 15: 7 by the words, 'Ye shall ask
what ye will, and it shall be done unto you.'

It is conceivable that there will be various reactions to
these statements. There will, no doubt, be those who will
dismiss them as being too fantastic or unrealistic and
therefore reject them altogether. Some, probably, will rub
their hands together gleefully, believing they are on to a
good thing without giving due consideration to what is
stated, and the result will be disappointment and frustration. Others will accept the truth and understand the
spiritual meaning, and therefore experience what is
promised.

Notice carefully what is stated and it will be discovered
that it is a promise in the very terms of the precept. For
our enlightenment it may be paraphrased: 'Delight in the
Lord and thou mayest trust thy desires; they will be the
forerunner of blessings, the beginnings of their own realisation.' When a man delights in God, his desires are of
such a nature that God would be glorified in granting
them and the man himself benefited by receiving them.

14

The promise is not given indiscriminately to all and sundry. It would be calamitous for the world if God gave all men the desires of their hearts without giving due consideration to the nature of a man's heart. Man is basically selfish, consequently his desires can be indulgent and whimsical. For instance, a man might request the quenching of a volcano or the arresting of the flow of a river of lava, but the granting of such a desire might cause a terrible earthquake in some vastly populated area and bring death and destruction to thousands of people.

The key to this promise is in the little word 'delight'. What does this mean? In a practical way it is delighting in the service of God and in the fellowship of God's people; having pleasure in reading and studying His Word and being in communion with Him; delighting in submitting completely to Him, as it says in Psalm 40: 8, 'I delight to do thy will, O my God.' When the people of God find happiness in doing these things they are then in a condition of soul that what they ask will be granted!

The Lord Jesus Christ also clarifies the point by putting a condition on the promise when He said, 'If ye abide in me, and my words abide in you, ye shall ask what ye will, and it shall be done unto you.' The trouble with most of us is that we are not spiritually prepared along this line and therefore our requests are often carnal and we ask 'amiss.'

This promise shows the extent to which God will answer the requests of His people who are fully surrendered to Him. No wonder David cried, 'Create in me a clean heart, O God; and renew a right spirit within me' (Ps. 51: 10). When the heart is right, we may enter into the glorious realm of this promise.

6 Victory over Satan

Resist the devil, and he will flee from you.
James 4: 7

Some years ago I overheard a conversation which two
people were having about Satan. One said that he was not
at all worried about him as he did not believe that he
existed or, if he did, then he must be chained up. 'In that
case,' said the other, 'he must be on a long chain!' A
rather humorous but significant reply. The biblical view
about the arch-enemy of the Church of Christ is stated in
no uncertain terms.

It is rather amazing that we hear very little about the
Devil when the Bible speaks so much about him. No less
than eighteen major titles are ascribed to him, including
the 'Prince of the devils' (Matt. 12: 24); the 'Prince of the
power of the air' (Eph. 2: 2); the 'Prince of this world'
(John 14: 30). His work is devoted to the destruction of all
that is good. We read that he 'beguiled' Eve, 'tempted'
David, 'hindered' Paul. Jesus made his aims crystal clear
when he said, 'The thief cometh to steal, and to kill, and
to destroy' (John 10: 10). He wages constant all-out war
against the Church of God, adopting various tactics to
bring about her downfall.

Satanic attack is not confined to open and direct assault;
he often achieves his purposes by flattering promises or
through the fascination of worldly things and we must
ever be on our guard against his deceptive strategy. Sometimes he withdraws all opposition. This often proves more
effective, resulting in Christians becoming negligent about
their spiritual exercises, with disastrous results. It is true
what Bishop Hall said on one occasion, 'Satan rocks the
cradle when we sleep at our devotions.' How many there

16

are today in the sleep of death who were caught unawares by the cunning machination of Apollyon.

The promise is, however, that we can defeat him! The secret of how we may do this is very largely found in the little word 'resist'. The NEB translated this verse as 'Stand up to the devil and he will turn and run!' See also Ephesians 6:11. Whether he uses temptation or threats we must manfully resist him.

The trouble with most of us is we succumb too readily to moods of depression, because of adverse circumstances, unkind criticisms and the like. We fail to see that, behind most of these things, a sinister power is at work to thwart the plan of God for our lives. We are exhorted to throw off the mantle of gloom which the Devil delights to place upon the people of God. Instead of living in despair like the defeatists of old who hung their harps upon the willows, we may experience complete victory and cry exultingly like Paul, 'In all these things we are more than conquerors through him that loved us' (Rom. 8:37).

When our lives are fully yielded to God, and Spirit-filled, we resist the forces of evil with the Word of God as Jesus did. Then there will be no cause for alarm. We will triumph over every evil force. Tyron Edwards wrote, 'The Devil has at least one good quality, that he will flee if we resist him – though cowardly in him it is safety for us.'

This is not the prerogative of a few select saints. The fascinating prospect for all the people of God is that they can be amongst the company of whom the Bible says 'Ye have overcome the wicked one.' Timid child of God, fear not, rise up in the strength of God, challenge the awesome enemy and prevail! You will prove the words of Ralph Waldo Emerson to be true. 'Do the thing you fear and the death of fear is certain.' More than this, the promise is that the foe will turn and run!

7 The Burden Bearer

Cast thy burden upon the Lord, and he shall sustain thee. Psalm 55:22

The world is full of people carrying burdens of some kind or other; care, toil, affliction, loss, weakness, poverty and such like. Generally speaking, our burdens are either physical, social, spiritual or mental. Multitudes of weary folk are in need of relief in so many ways. The wonderful thing about the Gospel is that it carries good news for all who are oppressed and suffering under the strain and stress of life. The Saviour, in His day, looked upon the masses: He saw them bowed down with their load of guilt and anxieties and was moved with compassion. He cried, 'Come unto me all ye that labour and are heavy laden, and I will give you rest' (Matt. 11:28). This gives us an insight into the yearning heart of God. He longs to help the downcast! What relief would come our way if we would only listen to His voice and accept His offer instead of trying to struggle through life by our own efforts.

The invitation here is for everyone to unload their burden on Him. His back is broader and stronger than ours! His strength is infinite. He who upholds 'all things by the word of his power' (Heb. 1:3) and is able to hang the earth on nothing, can certainly deal with our situation! The point is, are we willing to 'cast' our cares upon Him? The text implies that He is near enough to us to do this. 'The Lord is at hand.' We pray and sigh about our troubles, we resolve to cast them upon the Lord, but we don't do it. When we get off our knees we take our burdens back again. We often lack the childlike faith to believe that each day He is waiting to give the helping hand.

There are two ways whereby God can assist us. One is

by removing the thing which is intolerably heavy and crushing and, secondly, by giving the necessary strength to bear the load. There is a sense in which every man must bear his own burden. God knows how to deal with us. He never makes a mistake. A Christian who has lost a loved one cannot have the weight of grief entirely removed, but he need not be overwhelmed by it. The rendering of the Amplified Version is helpful here. It reads 'releasing the weight of it.' That is, letting God take a hand to relieve the pressure from us. While the burden is not removed, He makes it easier to bear and imparts the necessary strength to carry on.

When we come to this place of surrender we will enjoy the benefit of the word 'sustain'. This is a priceless word of most comforting content. There are various shades of meaning to it. One conveys the thought of the ministry of a nurse. This means that God is ready to care tenderly for us as a nurse does for infants. He will be to us as a mother. It also has in it the suggestion of food. Burdened men are generally weary, with drooping spirits. But He waits at hand to meet our need, to feed us with the bread of life, to increase our vitality, to satisfy the soul and to put a song in the heart. This word also has a further meaning of 'support'. He is able to keep us from stumbling. He who can deal with my problem can take care of me also and carry me if need be! How true it is that 'He shall never suffer the righteous to be moved.'

Remember, also, this is a personal message. Notice it says 'thy burden'. God is interested in us as individuals. There is nothing too big for Him to tackle; nothing too small for Him to notice. When each individual soul is ready to call and act upon the Word the promise of being sustained will be made good.

8 Persecution Promised

*Yea, and all that will live godly in Christ
Jesus shall suffer persecution.*
2 Timothy 3: 12

Here is a promise that will not be found in any promise box! It is one, however, to which we need to give diligent attention. It may alarm some who think that to be a follower of Christ is all sunshine and song, to discover that true Christians who are promised peace and joy and life can also expect hatred and opposition. Christianity predicts for its followers that which would keep most men from embracing it – persecution. Yet millions of people continue to accept the claims of Christ upon their lives.

Jesus made it clear to His disciples that He was sending them forth as sheep in the midst of wolves (Matt. 10: 16). He told them that it was not going to be easy to follow Him. Yet He promised a special blessing for the tested and tried (Matt. 5: 11, 12). 'Blessed are ye, when men shall revile you, and persecute you, and shall say all manner of evil against you falsely, for my sake. Rejoice, and be exceeding glad: for great is your reward in heaven: for so persecuted they the prophets which were before you.' This is why Paul could exclaim, 'Therefore I take pleasure in infirmities, in reproaches, in necessities, in persecutions, in distresses for Christ's sake: for when I am weak, then am I strong' (2 Cor. 12: 10).

This, then, is something we can expect as we walk the pilgrim pathway. Phillip's translation of the text makes this very clear to us. 'Persecution is inevitable for those who are determined to live really Christian lives.'

This was true of all the giants of the Bible. They willingly suffered for God, knowing it was a part of His divine plan. They knew all the degrees of persecution, from fiery

20

stake to scornful sneer. They had the courage to face every test and came through with a song of triumph in their hearts.

Recently, in America, I met a famous preacher. He stated that his godly father had said to him on one occasion, 'It takes grit as well as grace to sing praises at midnight. I know grit is not a very pretty word, but it denotes an excellent quality. It is that percentage of iron in a man's temperament that gives stability and permanence to his character – a steel rod in his backbone.' The trouble with a lot of us is, we lack grit. We need the same spiritual anointing as the early Church experienced. When we receive this, we will have the power to face any foe.

In a way, persecution is as necessary as the sun and rain. It does something for us which nothing else can. Someone once said, 'A genuine Christian is something like the firmament, and it is the blackness of affliction that makes his starry graces shine out. He is like those herbs and plants that best effuse their odours when bruised.' It seems the greater the persecution the more the early Church believers excelled in Christian character. That is why Peter said, 'If any man suffer as a Christian, let him not be ashamed; but let him glorify God on this behalf'. (1 Peter 4: 16).

The picture of the Church in the New Testament is one that shows her in the midst of constant attack, harassed, hated, despised, as Jesus predicted, but coming out of the fiery trial victorious and defying all the forces of evil to do their worst. Paul speaks for the early Church believers when he writes in Romans 8: 35-37, 'Who shall separate us from the love of Christ? shall tribulation, or distress, or persecution, or famine, or nakedness, or peril or sword? . . . Nay, in all these things we are more than conquerors through Him that loved us.' I wonder how many of us would speak with the same conviction today if we were faced with similar circumstances.

9 The Living Word

So shall my word be that goeth forth out of my mouth: it shall not return unto me void, but it shall accomplish that which I please, and it shall prosper in the thing whereto I sent it. Isaiah 55: 11

Many preachers and Sunday school workers who have faithfully laboured in teaching the Word of God, with very few visible results, have found encouragement in promises such as this one. The particular promise we are considering is enhanced by the fourfold 'shall'. It gives wonderful scope for the exercise of faith.

We must always remember that we are not only expected to sow the good seed of the Word but are exhorted to anticipate a harvest, to believe that our labour in this direction is not in vain in the Lord. The assurance given is, 'It shall prosper in the thing whereto I sent it.' Verse 10 points out that as the rain sinks into the ground and stimulates the grain, resulting in seed to the sower and bread to the eater, similarly the Word of God, when assimilated into the human mind fashions thought, moulds character and generates life.

It has divine power in it and therefore must produce a good effect in the lives of those who accept it. 'The entrance of Thy words giveth light; it giveth understanding unto the simple,' says the Psalmist (Ps. 119: 130). On the other hand, it is never 'void' even when it is rejected by the hardened sinner. It leaves them without excuse and seals their condemnation. Gospel preaching to crowds of unregenerate people who spurn its invitation can never be said to be a 'waste of time'. There is an all-wise purpose even in that. What a responsibility rests upon us all to present the truth with forcefulness, clarity and with love.

But how thrilling it is to see this word taking root and bringing forth fruit in men's hearts. I read recently of a Christian worker who gave a booklet to a young man. As he handed it to him he expressed his desire for the young man's salvation. When the Christian had departed the young man threw the booklet into the fire. As the pages curled up in the flame, his eye caught the words, 'Heaven and earth shall pass away, but my words shall not pass away' (Matt. 24: 35). As these words turned to ashes in the fire, they turned to fire in his mind. The result was that he surrendered his life to God and became a fruitful committed believer.

Testimonies like this could be repeated thousands of times over. What a great move forward would be experienced in the Church if we gave more attention to 'spreading the Word.' The Hebrew word 'prosper' literally means 'pushes forward'. It is a great dynamic force. The Bible is a living book because it is God's book. It is the Word of His mouth. The Scriptures assert that God is profoundly concerned for all mankind to read and accept if they will.

It is significant to note that practically every revival has been preceeded by a study of an obedience to the Word of God and, incidentally, such a move has inevitably been followed by a proclamation of the truth. It is a healthy sign to see, in the activities of the local church, prominence given to the Scriptures. Blessed is the church of whom it can be said, 'for from you is sounded out the Word of God.' This is the New Testament pattern for progress. Let us all be faithful heralds of the Living Word.

10 A Secure Future

Commit thy way unto the Lord; trust also in him; and he shall bring it to pass.
Psalm 37:5

Frequently in the Bible life is compared to a journey, a way, a road. All true believers are as pilgrims travelling on a road leading from the city of darkness to the celestial city of light. But the way is beset with dangers and, alas, it is not a straight pathway; there are gradients and declines and bends that can be frightening. I met a lady some time ago who was terrified to walk alone over the brow of a hill because of what she might meet on the other side. There are many on the journey of life like her who are gripped by fear because they do not know the road ahead. The prospect of an uncertain future fills them with gloom.

The true believer, however, need not have any such fears for he can exclaim confidently, as one of old, 'He knoweth the way that I take.' We are exhorted in this verse to 'commit' our way or affairs to Him. In the margin of some Bibles we read, 'Roll thy way upon the Lord.' The image here is of one rolling off from his shoulders a burden which he is not able to bear, on to one who is well able to bear it.

Many people worry about what they may meet on life's journey. Some get depressed and give up the struggle. But the promise here is most encouraging for all who are wondering what is going to happen to them. Recently, I read a translation that makes the point clearer. It is, 'Commit thy future unto the Lord, trust also in Him and He will work it out.' What is needed, then, is simple, childlike trust in God to believe that 'all things work together for good to them that love God, to them who are the called according to his purpose' (Rom. 8: 28).

We must cease fretting about tomorrow. The point is, are we willing to commit our future to Him? Are we ready to submit to His plans? The trouble with most of us is that we are bent on going our own way and mapping out our own road ahead. We are so busy with our own planning we cannot hear the voice of the Lord saying, 'This is the way, walk ye in it' (Is. 30: 21). We think we know better and this leads inevitably to the place of despondency. Many have discovered the folly of trying to run their own lives.

Here we have a gracious invitation. Instead of trying to live beyond what we are capable of doing and endeavouring to scheme at ways and means of meeting any difficult situation, we are offered a helping hand. We are told that HE WILL WORK IT OUT, solve our problems and meet our need.

From the start there is no need to walk alone. He begins the journey of life with us as soon as we invite Him to come. He is with us now and there is one thing of which we can be sure about the future – God will be there! If we let Him take over we will lose nothing. He can do more for us than we can do for ourselves, that's for sure. Martin Luther once wisely remarked, 'I have tried to keep things in my own hands, and I have lost them all, but what I have given into God's hands I still possess.'

Let us then hand over our tomorrow to Him and we can be certain that at the end of the journey everything will work out for His glory and our eternal benefit. If we let Him take control the reward is sure and the way will be glorious.

11 The Promise of Restoration

I will heal their backsliding, I will love them
freely: for mine anger is turned away from
him. Hosea 14: 4

Backsliding in the Bible is expressed in various ways –
falling, departing, forgetting, forsaking, denying God, and
so on. In some respects the backslider is in a worse predicament than those who have never known Christ. It is a
perilous position to be in. It seems that in this condition
the conscience becomes 'seared'. The eyes totally blind to
the things of God and the ears doubly deaf to the voice of
God. A backsliding heart is the worst of all spiritual
diseases.

It is interesting, however, to observe that several of the
most outstanding saints in the Bible, at some time in their
lives, turned away from God and disgraced His name.
Peter forsook the Saviour and he swore on oath that he
never knew Jesus. His blasphemous lies brought upon
him that suffering which is felt probably more heavily
than anything – remorse. The Scripture says, with alarm-
ing poignancy, he 'went out, and wept bitterly.' David
the king committed adultery and then murdered to try to
cover up his sin! He, too, knew the anguish of heart that
results from forsaking the way of righteousness and cried,
'My sin is ever before me.'

But for Peter in the New Testament, as for David in the
Old, there was forgiveness. Whereas their evil deeds could
not be erased from the memory, they were not prevented
from having communion with God, and afterwards
achieving great things for God.

How wonderful to know there can be restoration for
the prodigals who have wandered into the 'far country'.
Even those who have deliberately gone into sin with their

eyes open may return. This word 'backsliding' here really means apostasy, not merely an occasional slip back. This is what caused Calvin to exclaim, 'God can heal the most desperate sinfulness.' Yes, He loves them freely. His is a gratuitous, unmerited, abundant love that reaches to the uttermost extremities of human need.

That God is very much concerned about those who have gone astray cannot be denied. At least three books in the Bible are especially addressed to backsliders; two in the Old Testament and one in the New Testament. In Jeremiah the word 'backsliding' occurs more times than in any other book. Hosea is known as the 'Gospel of backsliders.' In Galatians Paul writes about the foolish believers who had been 'bewitched' and 'so soon removed'. In all three volumes the offenders are urged to return to the fold where a welcome awaits them. This thought inspired Samuel Davies to write, 'But countless acts of pardoning grace beyond thine other wonders shine: Who is a pardoning God like Thee? Or who has grace so rich and free?'

All that is needed for God's anger to be 'turned away' is to genuinely repent, as Israel did. How speedily God answered their prayer of self condemnation. It brought forth the ready response from the heart of God, 'I will heal' and 'I will love'. The hymn-writer expressed it perfectly when he wrote, 'Love only waits to forgive and forget; home! weary wanderer, home!' Furthermore, God's forgiveness is complete; He will never incriminate the pardoned soul.

The story is told of a king who had suffered much from his rebellious subjects. One day they surrendered their arms, threw themselves at his feet and begged for mercy. He pardoned them all. Then one of his friends said to him, 'Did you not say that every rebel should die?' 'Yes,' replied the king, 'but I see no rebels there.' Our heavenly Father is just like that!

12   Fruitfulness Promised

*They that sow in tears shall reap in joy. He
that goeth forth and weepeth, bearing
precious seed, shall doubtless come again
with rejoicing, bringing his sheaves with him.*
Psalm 126: 5-6

This promise to God's ancient people holds good for the Church today. The same principles apply – 'We shall reap, if we faint not' (Gal. 6: 9). It is a promise that should excite believers to participate in the most noble work of all, that of sowing the seed of divine truth in the hearts of unregenerate men.

We are all called to broadcast the Word of Life, but it is to be regretted that this is a neglected work, perhaps because of a feeling of unworthiness on the part of some. Many put forward the plea that they are too timid; others seem to adopt a 'couldn't care less' attitude to this great mission that is nearest and dearest to the heart of the Saviour.

These excuses and lack of concern grieve the Holy Spirit and result in spiritual barrenness to the Church.

Maybe it is the hardness of the way that causes most Christians to evade this vocation. Here we have the picture of a farmer who is weary, going forth scattering the seed and weeping with disappointment, but he perseveres. This is a type of the true believer who persists in spite of set-backs and heartaches. When God's blessing is upon a man it does not mean that he is exempt from tears. It is inevitable that he will have his seasons of sorrow. Sighing is as much a part of the divine pattern as is sunshine. It is often necessary that our hearts be broken before we can see the hearts of sinners break.

William Booth was approached one day by one of his followers, who reported that the work was difficult and he wasn't getting anywhere. He asked his leader what he could do. The General replied, 'TRY TEARS.'

We should never be ashamed to weep. Melted hearts are necessary in this 'sowing' business. Weeping is a sublime form of worship. Tears are often more eloquent than words. We are closer to the Saviour when we weep than when we work. Jesus Himself was 'acquainted with grief'. Three times we are told that He wept. This is not merely emotional or sentimental weeping. It is because of deep concern for men, a desire to do God's will and the realisation that apart from Him we can do nothing.

But here we have a most heartening promise. There is much cause for rejoicing. The continued perseverance of the sower will bring its reward. We can be sure that God has kept an exact register of our every effort to promote His kingdom and it will receive a recompense that is proportionate to its zeal and sincerity. The matter is settled and the faithful will be compensated. The sob will give place to the song.

The promise is, 'Shall doubtless come again with rejoicing,' and we have the analogy of nature to assure us of it. The great C. H. Spurgeon once said, 'I cannot comprehend anyone trying to win souls and being satisfied without results.' Generally speaking, most workers see the results of their labours.

However, in some cases it may appear that all efforts have proved ineffectual. Loved ones may still be outside the fold and all toil seems in vain. But God has guaranteed to give the 'increase'. He will cause the seed that has been sown to burst into life and bring it to fruition in His time. This may happen long after the sower has gone to be with the Lord. One thing is certain for all sowers, the harvest time will come, the sheaves will be gathered in. Every good work will bring its own benediction. Let us not be downcast. The road may be rough and long and dark, but remember, 'Weeping may endure for a night, but joy cometh in the morning' (Ps. 30: 5).

13 The Father's House

In my Father's house are many mansions:
if it were not so, I would have told you. I go
to prepare a place for you. John 14: 2

Is there anything beyond the grave? This is a question that man has grappled with for ages. The philosophers of the world, both ancient and modern, have propounded their ideas on the subject, but they amount to only vague speculations spoken with an uncertain sound. Many of the great religious leaders have been strangely silent on this important matter. Their gospel offers guidance chiefly for this life only.

Christ, however, speaks with a boldness and clarity on this theme that demands the attention of all. He never leaves us in doubt concerning the most important things. Jesus made some amazing, forthright, dogmatic pronouncements about Himself, judgment, sin, Hell and Heaven, and so on. We have to accept them or reject them. They are either true or not true. There can be no compromise. If Christ can be proved wrong on one point, then He can be wrong on other important issues, but 'no man spake like this man.' His doctrine has stood the test of time and He stands unsurpassed as the greatest teacher who cannot be ignored without tremendous loss to ourselves.

Christ's authoritative declarations about the abode of saints beyond the grave have stumbled many and have caused an offence to some but, at the same time, they have brought comfort to millions of true believers. Our Lord repeatedly spoke about the heavenly home, i.e. Matthew 25: 31 and 34; John 17: 24, 18: 36 and 14: 1-3. It is a place of rest, purity and peace, where the redeemed will enjoy perennial youth, sin will be banished, sorrow and sighing will be no more. It will be the great paradise of God.

In the Bible we have a number of descriptions of Heaven. It is described as a 'kingdom' (Eph. 5: 5 and 2 Peter 1: 11), a 'better country,' or, literally, 'a fatherland' (Heb. 11: 16), also 'city' (Heb. 11: 10), and, of course, as we have in our text, it is called the 'Father's house' in which there are many mansions.

The most important factor, of course, for our consideration is, how we get there. Here again Jesus emphatically stated, 'I am the way,' and added, 'No man cometh unto the Father, but by me.' One poor, illiterate fellow put it this way, 'It's a very simple way to Heaven,' he said. 'There are only three steps. Out of self – into Christ – into glory.'

'Oh, what a glorious personal promise from the Saviour this is. 'I go to prepare a place for you,' and the amazing thing is we have done nothing to deserve it. Someone made a rather significant statement when he declared, 'There will be three things which will surprise us when we get to Heaven. One, to find many there that we did not expect to find there. Another, to find some not there that we had expected. The third, and perhaps the greatest one, will be to find ourselves there.' It is true to say that the privilege of going to Heaven is the highest possible destiny and the greatest blessing that can be bestowed upon an individual. The child of God facing eternity need not fear. Revelation 14: 13 endorses the promise of Christ, 'And I heard a voice from heaven saying unto me, Write, Blessed are the dead which die in the Lord from henceforth: Yea, saith the Spirit, that they may rest from their labours; and their works do follow them.'

Of course, the wonderful fact about the Christian experience is that we may enjoy a foretaste of heaven here and now. As we get to know Christ in intimate fellowship

and trust Him implicitly to lead the way, we will experience an 'earnest of our inheritance'. The hymn-writer
puts it like this, 'On land or sea, what matters where,
Where Jesus is 'tis heaven there.'

14   No More Tears

*God shall wipe away all tears from their
eyes.* Revelation 7: 17

Some time ago, I received a letter from a Christian lady
who was passing through a time of deep sorrow. In addi-
tion to losing her son a few years before, she was now bereft of her daughter, aged twenty-one, who had died from
cancer. She was naturally feeling the blow of this double
tragedy and was burdened down with grief that was hard
to bear. Her letter was almost apologetic because she was
reduced to tears and missing her daughter so terribly.

Is it wrong to mourn when our loved ones are taken
from us? Surely not. It would be unnatural if we did not
grieve. Weeping is a God-given safety valve to bring relief
to our pent-up emotions. Tears are an effectual balm and
help to soothe and heal the wounded heart. Furthermore,
it is surely a great consolation to the sorrowing soul to
know that God is never more near to us than when we are
broken and crushed and melted. It is at times like these
that our vision of God becomes more vivid. As Browning
declares:

> 'Thank God for grace, ye who only weep!
> If, as some have done,
> Ye grope tear blinded in a desert place,
> And touch but tombs, look up! and thus
> Tears will run
> Soon in long rivers down the lifted face,
> And leave the vision clear for stars and sun.'

There is a danger, of course, that we have to guard
against; that is to lament beyond what is legitimate and
good for us, like 'Rachel weeping for her children, and

would not be comforted.' When this happens we frustrate the purpose of God in our lives and this certainly would not be the wish of those for whom we grieve.

But how can one find comfort and strength to carry on at a time of great sorrow? First of all, in the realisation that others too are travelling with us through this vale of tears. We are not alone in our sorrow. It is helpful to note also that some of the greatest saints in the Bible were at times brokenhearted. In Genesis 23: 2, Abraham felt keenly the loss of his wife, Sarah, and wept. Then there is a very moving scene in Genesis 50: 1. Jacob had died and Joseph was overcome with grief. The Bible says, 'And Joseph fell upon his father's face, and wept upon him, and kissed him.' It will assist us greatly to study how they carried on their daily tasks in spite of anguish of soul.

Remember also that our Lord was 'acquainted with grief' all through His earthly ministry. He was sent for the express purpose of healing the brokenhearted (Luke (4: 18). He Himself suffered the agonies of human distress. Three times it is stated that Jesus wept; i.e. over Jerusalem (Luke 19: 41); at the grave of Lazarus (John 11: 35); and in Hebrews 5: 7, where it says that Christ, during His earthly ministry, 'offered up prayers and supplications with strong crying and tears.' What a happy thought to know that Jesus, who knows the deepest woes of every person, 'ever liveth to make intercession for them'!

The ultimate comfort of the children of God, of course, is to know that Heaven is a place where God shall wipe away all tears because 'the former things have passed away.' That means the old order of things is superseded by the divine plan. No more death, sorrow, crying, pain, partings. The poet Burns said he could never read this without resorting to weeping with joy! Of all the negative descriptions of Heaven this is probably the most glorious and brings the greatest consolation.

To the children of God, amidst the trials of this present

35

life, we have the privilege of looking beyond the grave to the brighter hope of Heaven and home. When we contemplate that this is a place where tears shall be wiped away, the prospect of such a world should contribute to wipe away our tears here and make our burden easier to bear, for in that land we will meet to part no more.

15 Dependable

For all the promises of God in him are yea,
and in him Amen, unto the glory of God
by us. 2 Corinthians 1: 20

In these days of turmoil and worldwide unrest when it seems that the ungodly are 'flourishing like the green bay tree', the child of God can so easily be plunged into the depths of despair and wonder if God is working out His purposes. How quickly we subject ourselves to the taunts of the Devil in thinking we are forsaken of the Lord. We can sympathise with those who are passing through a severe test and are tempted, like the Psalmist, to cry, 'Is his mercy clean gone forever? Doth his promise fail for evermore?' (Ps. 77: 8).

It is at times such as these that we need to remind ourselves of the dependability of the promises of God. The triumphant song of S. C. Kirk still holds good today, one verse of which is:

'The Lord hath declared, and the Lord will perform:
    Behold I am near to deliver,
A refuge and fortress, a covert in storm; He keepeth
    His promise for ever!
For ever, for ever! Oh, not for a day! He keepeth
    His promise for ever!
To all who believe, to all who obey, He keepeth His
    promise for ever! '

The verse under consideration refers to all that is promised in Christ, including forgiveness of sin, sanctification of the children of God, power for service, victory over temptation, peace in the storm, guidance that is sure and a glorious hope beyond the grave. All these things are as sure as God exists.

37

Notice the 'Yea' – this word is to emphasise the fact that there will be no vacillation on God's part. He is not fickle like man. The NEB puts it, 'He is the Yes pronounced upon God's promises, every one of them.' Observe also the important word 'Amen', which means true, faithful, certain.

The 'Yea, and 'Amen' to the promises of God is a profound and magnanimous declaration. We have here the immutable verification of them. Oh, what comfort and cheer for all believers to know that God in Christ makes the fulfilment of these promises doubly sure. He gives us the assurance that He will keep His word in the 'Yea' and confirms it with an oath in the 'Amen'! Can anything be more reassuring than this?

Old and New Testament promises are secure and the fulfilment of them is vouchsafed to us in Christ our Saviour. What we must bear in mind, of course, is that it is only as we 'abide in Christ' (see John 15) can we continue to enjoy these things for ourselves. It is one thing to have a revelation of all that we need and to see that all is supplied in Christ, but it is another thing to experience them in our own lives. Daily walking with Him is the answer.

Very often I get letters bearing testimony to the validity and fulfilment of God's promises. Here is an example from an aged Christian, 'I am in my eighty-first year and the Lord has been all that He promised for 62 years.' Recently I read that in the margin of the Bible used by evangelist D. L. Moody there were the letters 'T' and 'P' on almost every page. He was asked one day what those letters meant. He replied by saying that each passage contained a promise of God to His children. The 'T' indicated that he had tried the promise and the 'P' meant that he had proved the promise to be true in his own experience.

The children of God throughout every generation have been quick to acclaim the faithfulness of God in times of trial. As we meditate on this text our hearts surely are filled with deep gratitude to Him who has condescended to speak to His people to guarantee what He has pledged. Every true believer can look up into the face of our Heavenly Father and say with real conviction and holy joy:

' 'Tis true, O, yes 'tis true, God's wonderful promise is true,
For I've trusted, and tested, and tried it. And I know God's promise is true! '

16 · Ask and Receive

Ask, and it shall be given you; seek, and ye shall find; knock, and it shall be opened unto you. Matthew 7: 7

Thomas à Kempis said on one occasion that it is a great art to commune with God. Few of us, so it seems, have learned and applied the principles of effective prayer.

Yet all the children of God have an open invitation to the throne of grace, not only for the privilege of 'waiting' in His presence and worshipping the Lord, but to ask for needs to be met (Phil. 4: 19), desires to be granted (Ps. 37: 4), and for the purposes of God to be worked out in our lives after the counsel of His will (Eph. 1: 11).

Real praying is expressed in the terms ask, seek and knock, words of unimitable simplicity, but of the utmost import. They represent a threefold action required to enable us to obtain the things we need from God. When we put them into operation we have a triple assurance from our Heavenly Father that He will grant that which is desired.

Now the promise is that if we ask, it shall be given. At first glance this appears to be an over-simplification to obtain the answer to our prayers. But we must fully understand what is meant by asking, otherwise there will be disappointment with regard to the receiving.

Many Christians do not enter into their full spiritual inheritance for the simple reason that they do not beseech God to meet their need on a particular line. James says, 'Ye have not, because ye ask not'. There are others who do not 'receive' because, as the same writer points out in 4: 3, they 'ask amiss', or, as the NEB puts it, 'Your requests are not granted because you pray from the wrong motives.' We must rid ourselves of all purely selfish desires if we want our prayer life to become fruitful. It is essential also when we pray to ask in faith. Jesus said, 'What things soever ye desire, when ye pray, believe that ye receive them, and ye shall have them' (Mark 11:24).

We see also an important truth in this word 'seek'. It means we must be serious, keen and ardent in our supplications. True prayer is an intense, heartfelt operation. Every promise is attached to a duty, but it is not enough that we do it, we must do it scripturally. The promise is not made good to those who only seek, but to those who seek God with all their heart.

Then, thirdly, the knocking represents perseverance and regularity. Keeping on until the answer comes, just like the man in the gospels who wanted loaves of bread for his friend (Luke 11:5), and like Elijah in 1 Kings 18:44, who prayed on until the rain came. In both cases it required determination. How often we fail to make the promises good in our lives because we are not constant. We give up too readily.

It is a happy coincidence that in our English Bible the first letters of each word under consideration, when put together, spell out the significant syllable 'Ask'! What an encouragement this promise is for all God's people who are feeling downhearted and frustrated. The Almighty can make the valley of Achar become a door of hope; the wilderness a pool and the desert to blossom as the rose! Nothing is too hard for the Lord and the invitation is extended to all to come to the One who can do the impossible and ask for deliverance. He is ready to give 'beauty for ashes, the oil of joy for mourning, the garment of praise for the spirit of heaviness' (Is. 61:3).

And, remember, we are not to ask as beggars and vagabonds, but as children who are heirs to the wealth of God's boundless resources! What we must constantly

41

keep in mind, of course, is that these things are only for those whose prayer life combines this threefold form of asking wisely, seeking earnestly and knocking persistently.

17 Christ in the Midst

*Where two or three are gathered together
in my name, there am I in the midst of
them.* Matthew 18: 20

This promise of Jesus is most interesting as it is set
against the background of activities and affairs of the
local Church. It is particularly helpful to us in these days
when it seems in a number of instances that the work of
God is about to disintegrate.

The word 'Ichabod', which means 'the glory has departed', can be written over the portals of many churches.
These drab, cold, uninviting edifices are matched by the
spiritual barrenness of their congregations within. World-
liness, unbelief and a subtle form of atheism have resulted
in the Church becoming a by-word to the ungodly and a
confused generation of 'Christian' young people crying,
'Where is the God of our fathers?'

When it seems that the majority have cast in their lot
with those who have compromised the truth to such an
extent that God is dethroned, Christ reduced to a mere
man and the Gospel made to appear meaningless, we are
apt to succumb to abject despair.

In the light of this tragic state of affairs, the promise
which Jesus Christ gives here is very encouraging. We
have reason to be hopeful for the cause is not entirely lost
so long as there remains a remnant of consecrated believers. If God can find 'two or three' faithful Christians
He will presence Himself among them and vindicate their
claim to the belief that the God of Abraham, Isaac and
Jacob is still on the throne!

It has always been the 'few' who have taken up the challenge of evil forces and stemmed the tide of carnality and

godlessness. Those brave people of God met together in homes and caves and catacombs to pray through to victory over the powers of darkness. In Wesley's day, the little groups of believers who gathered to study God's Word and to seek His help were sneered at and called 'Holy Clubs' and 'Methodists', but they were triumphant. They were instrumental in reviving the Church.

Dr. Torrey, the well-known preacher, once made a statement about revival that is worth noting, the substance of which I give here. 'I have a prescription for revival that I have given to God's people all over the world, and it has never failed. Firstly, let a company of Christians unite together; they need not be many. Secondly, let them get thoroughly right with God themselves, getting rid of any known sin. Then let them give themselves to unceasing prayer and be determined to pray through until the blessing comes. That is all.'

In this connection it is vitally important that we fully realise the significance of these words of the Saviour – 'In my name'. This is synonymous with saying, 'doing my will' or 'walking in my footsteps.' In other words, to meet together in the name of Christ is to be entirely in sympathy with Christ, to have the same spirit and disposition. Our Lord said, 'Whatsoever ye shall ask in my name, that will I do' (John 14: 13). He did not mean that all we have to do to get answers to prayer is simply to use the formula. Trust in and surrender to Christ are also implied and are necessary for the fulfilment of the promise.

Throughout the long history of the Church, God has invariably honoured the minority who refused to bow to sinister forces without and fifth-columnists within. Implicit faith in God's sovereignty and obedience to His Word inevitably brought a response from Him. Deadness gave way to Holy Ghost revival power; unbelief was confronted with apostolic miracles, atheism with a manifestation of the shekinah glory and, overall, the presence

44

of God brought conviction upon those who had strayed and caused many to cry out for mercy and restoration.

That we need another such demonstration of the presence of God goes without saying. The question is, are we prepared to so order our lives that this may be brought about?

18 Wisdom

If any of you lack wisdom, let him ask of
God, that giveth to all men liberally, and
upbraideth not; and it shall be given him.
James 1: 5

Let's face it, life is full of problems. Many things that happen we cannot understand and never will in this life. However, because we do not know the answer to a perplexing situation it does not mean there is none. It may well be that God, in His infinite love, deems it wise to hide some things from us on occasions because this is to our advantage. I wonder if, in our present state, it would contribute to our happiness if we knew what He knows?

Whereas knowledge is most useful, it also can lead us to greater problems as we in this space age well know. Our greatest need is not more knowledge, but wisdom. It would be wiser for us at times to be content with the knowledge that God knows all the facts and that He has the solution to that which appears to us at the present time a mystery.

Our existence may be compared to a work of art on tapestry. At the moment, what we gaze upon may appear to be meaningless, a tangled mess of broken or loose threads in various colours; a complex jigsaw puzzle conveying little. But when we get to Heaven we will behold the other side of the handiwork. Then will be revealed a glorious pattern of magnificent design. We shall see the finished work of incomparable artistic beauty woven by the divine hand. This will be the day of revelation, as Paul says in 1 Corinthians 13: 12, 'At present all I know is a little fraction of the truth, but the time will come when I shall know it as fully as God now knows me!' (Phillips.)

The promise of wisdom in this text is related mainly to our understanding this very point. Now we know a fraction of the truth; then the whole truth. In verse two, James says we can expect all kinds of trials and temptations as we go through life. We may have experiences that will leave us nonplussed, but, as Phillips puts it, 'If, in the process, any of you does not know how to meet any particular problem he has only to ask God . . . and he may be quite sure that the necessary wisdom will be given him.'

Many Christians will readily testify to receiving a word of wisdom from God after earnest prayer. Sometimes He inspires His people to take a firm line of action to solve a difficulty, or we may be led to be still and let God work out a problem in His time. Occasionally, He may give us the ability to perceive that a particular issue will not be fully solved here and that we should leave the matter in His hands. Wisdom sees beyond time to the day when all things will be worked out according to His eternal purpose and to our satisfaction.

Solomon said in Proverbs 4:7, 'Wisdom is the principal thing, therefore get wisdom.' It certainly is essential for us to possess this if we desire to live a spiritually contented life, unhampered by a fog of uncertainties. Note carefully then that we are invited to ASK for wisdom and the promise is that it will be given liberally in any given situation.

When we come to God about this matter, let us approach Him with boldness and confidence. We must not be half-hearted. Verses 6 and 7 tell us, 'But let him ask in faith, nothing wavering. For he that wavereth is like a wave of the sea driven with the wind and tossed. For let not that man think that he shall receive anything of the Lord.' The sad thing is that very few of us ask God for this, the greatest spiritual gift, which we so badly need and which He is so ready to give.

19 The Light of Life

I am the light of the world: he that
followeth me shall not walk in darkness,
but shall have the light of life. John 8: 12

It is most interesting to observe the occasion when Jesus made this profound statement. It was at a time when the Jewish 'feast of tabernacles' was being held, attended by our Lord. He spoke these words 'in the treasury' (verse 20) where, it is said, stood two huge columns about 'fifty cubits high', covered in gold. Hanging on these were numerous lamps which were lighted each evening of the feast, diffusing their brilliance over the city of Jerusalem. Around these the people joined in festive dances. The two colossal lampstands represented the pillar of cloud and of fire that shaded the Israelites by day and guided them by night in their journeyings in the wilderness.

But for centuries the glory had gone from the nation. They were, in fact, celebrating a departed Shekinah. They were living in the past. Their religious activities were reduced to empty ritual and dead formalism.

It was during some part of this feast that Christ, it is believed, pointed to the make-believe pillar of fire and cried, 'I am the light of the world.' Those present would realise the full significance of this statement. From henceforth the Son of Man would take the place of the pillar of fire and guide the people of God in their pilgrimage. The darkness of fear, ignorance, error, guilt and sin need not terrify them any longer. The Saviour had come to replace the symbol.

According to tradition, 'LIGHT' was one of the names of the Messiah and the promise Christ made was that all who

48

accepted Him 'shall have' the light of life; not look upon it from a distance, but receive it so that it becomes his own.

David knew about this experience when he said, 'The Lord is my light and my salvation; whom shall I fear? the Lord is the strength of my life; of whom shall I be afraid?' (Ps. 27: 1). In many places light is spoken of as a gift from God, but here it is not the gift, but God Himself who dispels the gloom!

This is exactly what transpires when we meet the conditions laid down by the Lord, 'He that followeth me.' The Phillips translation is, 'I am the light of the world. The man who follows me will never walk in the dark but will live his life in the light.'

Our understanding of the purposes of God becomes clear as we keep close to Him. We will not be left in uncertainty concerning His will for our lives; no black clouds of sin can envelop us if we dwell in His presence for 'God is light, and in Him is no darkness at all' (1 John 1: 5).

LIGHT, which is the emblem of knowledge, holiness and joy, is the promised reward for the children of God. What we need to realise, however, is the implication of the word 'followeth'. It can mean an awful lot at times to obey this injunction. To Paul, as others, it meant suffering, shipwreck, peril, privation, hunger, misunderstanding, and so on, but through it all the Lord stood by him and flooded his heart with cheer and radiancy.

It is important to bear in mind always that Jesus did not say, 'If you continue in my pathway you shall not walk into trouble and difficulties', but the assurance given is that we shall not walk alone in the darkness of utter despair. Solomon puts it like this: 'The path of the just is as the shining light, that shineth more and more unto the perfect day (Pro. 4: 18).

20   Renewed Strength

But they that wait upon the Lord shall renew their strength; they shall mount up with wings as eagles; they shall run, and not be weary; and they shall walk and not faint. Isaiah 40: 31

Do you ever feel spiritually fatigued and wonder if you will be able to carry on? Then do not be too despondent; many children of God have felt like that! Life can become terribly monotonous and burdensome; even Christian activity a wearisome task. Many a labourer has been left weeping with frustration and disappointment after years of faithful sowing have not yielded the eagerly anticipated bountiful harvest.

Often ministers of the Gospel have cried out from sheer exhaustion, 'Who is sufficient for these things?' But the God who has called us to live and work for Him has also provided the means to enable us to do His bidding. Paul found this to be true and wrote, 'Our sufficiency is of God' (2 Cor. 3: 5). He who commands also sustains.

In relationship to this promise we are invited to learn a lesson from the eagle. This majestic bird, although noted for strength, is not always strong. There is a season when it loses its feathers. At that time it sits solitary, drooping and sad, unable to rise to great heights. During that period, although incapable of flight towards the sun, it will bask in the sunshine until its feathers grow again; vitality returns and it is able to soar to the heavenlies.

Similarly, the children of God who 'wait upon the Lord shall renew their strength; they shall mount up with wings as eagles.' We become endued with power to rise above things. This is something we all need these days, so that we shall have a correct understanding of life and the purposes of God. Loftiness gives comprehension. To see things as we ought, we must get away from them. A trial looked at from below may be stupendous, but looked at from above it may appear to be a little thing for then we see how things are related to each other.

How wonderful it is that provision is made for the child of God to have these 'higher experiences'. We can manage to endure a great deal that is disagreeable and distressing if occasionally we can have seasons of spiritual uplift when we may be renewed in mind and body by the 'sun of righteousness'.

'They shall run, and not be weary' is also a wonderful part of this promise. Spurgeon once said, 'Scores of timid believers creep towards Heaven as the snail crept toward the ark.' This is not so with the trusting soul. He is like a marathon runner, not diminishing in strength, but rather quickening his pace. He is a runner who is in the race with the will to win the prize!

And what about the 'walking'? Whereas the 'heights' are for times of spiritual refreshment and the running depicts the urgency of the Christian life, walking is a picture of the plodding, diligent, persistent child of God. He will be given grace for the day-to-day tasks. He will 'not faint' is the emphatic declaration and is most reassuring.

It is important that we keep in mind that the fulfilment of this promise is dependent upon our obedience to that little word 'wait'. It means to look to God alone for inner renewal; to be calm and patient before Him and at the same time to EXPECT him to make good what He has decreed. The Psalmist had this thought in mind when he said, 'Wait on the Lord: be of good courage, and he shall strengthen thine heart: wait, I say, on the Lord' (Ps. 27: 14).

We miss a great deal when we are always on the go. Activity alone does very little to advance the kingdom of

God, indeed it can lead us into frustration and sometimes to defeat. We constantly require a supply of divine energy if we are going to be effective Christians. Let us then develop this holy habit of waiting on God and remember this is not so much a transient action as a permanent attitude.

21   The Brokenhearted

*The Lord is nigh unto them that are of a
broken heart; and saveth such as be of a
contrite spirit.* Psalm 34: 18

This Psalm opens with praise to God because of His
goodness. Much is said about the triumphs and blessings
of God's people. All through, the author rejoices for deliverance in the time of danger and his thanksgiving
reaches a mighty crescendo as he declares, 'they that seek
the Lord shall not want any good thing.' But what about
poor, dejected, afflicted sinners outside the fold who are
desirous of mending their ways and concerned about their
need? Is there any consolation for them?

In this verse we have the answer. God sees them in their
distress and is ready to help. In relationship to them, two
states are mentioned; a broken heart and a contrite spirit;
they often go together.

Here we have people who are in deep trouble; calamity
has overtaken them and left them shattered and helpless,
but not hopeless. However, much depends on how we re-
act to the tragedies and trials of life.

Sometimes as a result of tragedy, the heart becomes
hardened against the Almighty and a spirit of bitterness is
born, ripening into open rebellion. With others, it is the
opposite. Some are softened by sorrow and are receptive
to the message of salvation. Often when we are brought
low, we are more ready to listen, we become sensitive to
the wooing of the Holy Spirit and conscious of the near-
ness of God's presence.

When a man is bereft of loved ones and crushed under
a load of grief, he comes face to face with reality. Life is
then stripped of all delusions. He finds out who his real

53

friends are. True values are then discovered and he realises how insignificant he is. David knew something of this, and said in Psalm 39: 4-5, 'Lord, make me to know mine end, and the measure of my days, what it is; that I may know how frail I am. Behold, thou hast made my days as an handbreadth; and mine age is as nothing before thee: verily every man at his best state is altogether vanity.'

It is during moments like these that many realise for the first time that 'life is more than meat and drink' and the sorrowing soul suddenly finds the scales removed from his eyes and sees his own need.

It is often in the blackest hour we discover the most precious things. We cannot enjoy the grandeur of the stars unless we are prepared to walk in the dark. The child of God has been delivered from the darkness of sin and despair but he may often be led through times of mental and spiritual darkness which will result in his benefit. There is a wealth of meaning in the statement of the prophet Isaiah when he declared, 'I will give thee the treasures of darkness.' The stunning blow need not be taken as the signal that life has lost its meaning and that there must now follow a constant lament of utter hopelessness for the rest of the earthly pilgrimage. Rather, let it be a prelude to a new experience with God who can make all things work together for good.

Now notice the wonderful language here. 'The Lord is NIGH unto them.' God is in close proximity to the wounded heart. He waits eagerly to see what the reaction will be to the trial; contrition or induration, antagonism against God or acceptance of His offer of comfort and love.

When all self-asserting pride has been subdued and is replaced by humbleness of heart, then He comes to 'save' us from our fears and deliver us from our sins. A melted heart is the prerequisite for divine deliverance and God's benediction. Then He becomes a 'husband to the widow and a father to the fatherless'. Furthermore, He does not

54

draw near to us to pay a fleeting visit to offer His condolences, as is the wont of humans. He comes to say, 'I will never leave thee, nor forsake thee.' What the Psalmist says in this promise is amplified by Jesus in His sermon on the mount, when He declared, 'Blessed are they that mourn: for they shall be comforted' (Matt. 5: 4).

22 Palm Tree Christians

*The righteous shall flourish like the palm
tree: he shall grow like a cedar in Lebanon.*
Psalm 92: 12

'The righteous shall flourish.' That is the emphatic declaration of Holy Writ, it is the authoritative decree of the
Almighty, and in spite of whatever appears to the contrary,
this will be the happy lot of God's people. The gates of
Hell shall not prevail against the Church. She shall never
be vanquished but will flourish in the midst of a godless
world, as well as in the Courts of God. Evil forces will fin-
ally be thrown into disarray and defeated, for the battle is
the Lord's!

Notice the figure used here to describe the good for-
tunes of the godly. Their thriving and healthy state is
likened to the palm tree. This is a representative tree.
What the pine is to Canada and the oak to England, so
the palm tree is to the Church of God.

For usefulness it is unrivalled. Gibbon informs us that
the natives of Syria claimed it could be put to 360 uses!
Its verdure often springs from the scorching dust of the
desert. It stands – tall, majestic, beautiful; its leafy can-
opy and waving plumes are a cheery sight to the weary
travellers who rest under its shade. The naturalist informs
us that it bears an abundance of fruit because it is fed
from the hidden springs flowing beneath the surface of
the arid desert. Its roots drink deeply and are sustained.
Neither weight nor violence can stop this tree growing.
The more it is oppressed, the stronger and higher it grows.
What is more, it is evergreen.

What an emblem of the true saints of God! A picture
of dignity, usefulness and strength. In one of the ser-

mons of Dr Jowett, he described a Christian leader as 'A hiding place from the wind, a covert from the tempest; as rivers of water in a dry place, as the shadow of a great rock in a weary land.' What a boon the righteous have been in every generation.

Note the word 'righteous' and carefully consider the subject, for this is the key to the whole matter. It is used numerous times throughout the Bible to remind us of its importance.

God has made it crystal clear how we should live. Uprightness and loyalty, purity and fidelity are the virtues we must cultivate, but much of modern thinking rejects this way of life. Those who live to these standards leave themselves open to the sarcasm and scorn of those who ridicule biblical ethics, but the maxim that 'righteousness exalteth a nation' still holds good. This is not, of course, referring to self-righteousness, but the kind that Paul speaks of, 'not having mine own righteousness . . . but . . . the righteousness which is of God by faith' (Phil. 3: 9). This alone produces lasting and qualitative prosperity.

What encouragement and hope are expressed by the words of this promise! Nothing is more certain than the ultimate triumph of the godly who are referred to in Isaiah 61: 3 as 'trees of righteousness'. They will flourish like the palm and grow as the cedar.

Let not the faithful be despondent because of the present situation. It is wrong to draw conclusions from things as they seem at the moment. It looks as though irreligious and profane men are gaining ground, but mark the words of David, who uses the same simile of a tree to describe evil men – although note the difference, 'I have seen the wicked in great power, and spreading himself like a green bay tree. Yet he passed away, and, lo, he was not: yea, I sought him, but he could not be found' (Ps. 37: 35). How true it is that the pleasures of sin are only for a season.

The plain fact is that justice will prevail; the eternal counsels of God will never be thwarted. There is no need for any child of God to fear what the outcome is going to be as long as he follows 'righteousness, faith, charity, peace' (2 Tim. 2: 22) then the Lord of hosts will walk with us; the God of Jacob will be our refuge and this is the guarantee that we shall overcome.

23 No Condemnation

*None of them that trust in him shall be
desolate.* Psalm 34: 22

It is said that on the wall of one of the Egyptian pyra-
mids is written, 'The impious shall commit iniquity without recompense but not without remorse.' Millions of
transgressors, no doubt, would bear testimony to the
veracity of this statement.

Sin inevitably leads to moral desolation. When we stray
from the paths of righteousness the soul is alerted to the
realisation of wrong doing and the voice of conscience
speaks loud and clear, pronouncing the unmistakable
sentence of guilt.

Sin, of course, is not only a positive action, that is, vio-
lating the boundaries that God has set for our good, but it
is also a negative thing, a failure to live up to God's requirements.

Reactions to this state of condemnation are varied.
Some try to silence the accusing voice by vain arguments
and excuses; others by throwing overboard moral principles; and there are those who give themselves up to a life
of abandonment to vice. These actions serve only to increase the sense of incrimination, to enflame the passions,
to tighten the fetters of a soul in the dungeon of despair
until he cries out, like one of the great poets of the past
who lived a dissolute life, 'The worm, the canker, and the
grief are mine alone!' This unquestionably is the most
terrible form of desolation.

The sad thing is that man is all the time trying to free
himself. He is constantly endeavouring to produce an an-
tidote to rid him of his 'guilt complex' and fears, while at

the same time ignoring the one source that can bring him deliverance.

The wonderful news that the true Christian Church has to declare is that there is no need for man to sit any longer in darkness, terrified of the awful consequences of his actions.

Here in this text under consideration we have the Gospel message in the Old Testament, a 'blessed assurance' cast in negative form, but involving more than mere negation. The word 'desolate' has various shades of meaning, i.e. to incur guilt; to feel guilty; to be condemned; to be punished. All these are blended together in this word, making a fearful combination, but the promise is, we can be free from such thraldom, 'None of them that trust in Him shall be desolate.'

Could anything be more thrilling, comforting and hopeful than this to outcasts of society, to the weary and oppressed? All we are asked to do is to 'trust'. The Amplified Version makes this somewhat clearer. 'None of those who take refuge . . . in him shall be condemned.' The Psalmist on a number of occasions refers to God as a 'rock', one in whom we can hide, conveying the thought of security and peace. In Psalm 18:2 he declares, 'The Lord is my rock, and my fortress, and my deliverer; my God, my strength, in whom I will trust.' There we have a fairly comprehensive picture of how we may find deliverance.

Connected with, or flowing from, this act of trust is a glad surrender of self and a submission to God's will for our lives. When we do this we will experience the liberty of the sons of God. We shall indeed find the words of Jesus to be so true, 'If the Son therefore shall make you free, ye shall be free indeed' (John 8:36).

24 Faith Triumphant

Everything is possible to one who has faith.
Mark 9: 23 (NEB)

Here we have one of the profound statements of Jesus.
He makes known one of the great secrets of the kingdom.
The Master informs us that the key which opens the door
to achievement and conquest, provision and protection, is
faith.

There is no limit to what faith can accomplish. Nothing
can stand before it. The sea may roar its defiance against
men of God and the river overflow its banks, but faith
makes a way through the turbulent waters. Faith breaks
into the dungeons of doom and liberates the vice-bound,
devil-possessed outcasts. It gives strength to the weary and
hope to the hopeless.

Faith gives us wings to soar above all obstacles. It is
deaf to defeatist talk and blind to adverse circumstances.
It presses through all opposition to touch the hem of the
garment of the great physician, to receive divine healing
when all other sources have failed.

Faith sees the desert blossoming as the rose. It beholds
angelic hosts standing around enemy armies ready to take
them at His command. Faith marches on triumphantly;
no power can deter it, no decree can stop it.

Faith always ventures fearlessly into the unknown and
discovers new lands of promise. Faith has not, cannot,
will not, be vanquished. It is as enduring as love and hope
and constantly waves the flag of victory.

Faith is of heavenly origin. It is not produced by the
academies of men, either inside or outside the Church.
James writes, 'Every good gift and every perfect gift is

from above.' Faith is a gift from God, and one of the most blessed.

Faith is calm and resolute. It sits undisturbed among lions of prey. It sleeps like a babe in the face of the executioner's axe. In the vocabulary of faith's dictionary there are no such words or phrases as 'cannot', 'maybe', 'impossible', or 'we are not able'. The theme of the language of faith is 'Thanks be to God, which giveth us the victory!' It always encourages us to be 'more than conquerors'.

We do not need a 'lot of faith' or 'big' faith to see signs and wonders in our midst. If we possess just one grain of faith we will be able to move mountains of opposition from our path and 'nothing shall be impossible' (Matt. 17: 20 and 21).

The possibilities for one possessing faith are limitless. Without it we are ordinary men, with it we perform exploits and life takes on a new meaning. It becomes an apostolic adventure into the spiritual land of Canaan and takes it by storm, slays all giants, and then enjoys the grapes and the milk and the honey.

To qualify for faith we have to become as little children. It is not for 'know-alls' or for the worldly-wise, but for those with a simple childlike quality of belief. Except we become as little children we cannot enter into the Kingdom of Heaven. It is also true that unless we remain childlike in our belief we cannot enjoy the blessings of the kingdom.

Faith is not partial. It will blossom in the consecrated heart of a peasant, a priest or a prince. The prayer of us all should be, 'O, Lord, increase our faith.' Let us grasp this precious promise with both hands, fondle it tenderly, guard it securely, and repeat it continually, 'Everything is possible to one who has faith.'

25 God's Goodness

No good thing will he withhold from them
that walk uprightly. Psalm 84: 11

One of the facts that stands out when making a study
of the Bible is that God is concerned about the welfare of
His people. He has promised to strengthen, lead and pro-
vide for His own. Indeed, He will come to the aid of all
who call upon Him. This doesn't mean, of course, that life
will be a 'bed of roses' when a person becomes a Christian, or that God will grant everything we ask and satisfy
our every whim.

Earthly parents often act like this with such disastrous
results to their offspring. God cannot be charged with
such irresponsibility. It is not His intention to have a lot
of spoiled children in His kingdom. He is all wise and
knows that it would do us no good to have all that we desire.

When we walk with God, however, our hearts become
conditioned to asking according to His will. No one who
is surrendered to Him can make requests at the throne of
grace flippantly or selfishly. Such will know the mind of
the Lord and what they ask will be granted, bringing
abundant satisfaction.

Of course, many things may be denied to the faithful
children of God; but even this is to their advantage. The
promise here is, that 'no good thing will He withhold.'
This being so, it follows that what is withheld from us
would be of no use to us.

We are often confused in the understanding of the ab-
stract term 'good'. This is something that has intrinsic
value and is of a permanent nature. We cannot really de-
fine it unless we have experienced it. It is something in-

finitely more wonderful than the word itself suggests.

We may ask the question, 'Wherein lies lasting goodness?' We must not conclude that a thing is good unless we know its nature. An oak tree may to the casual observer look good, majestic and healthy, but often when the tempest rages through the forest such a tree is brought crashing to the ground, exposing its inner decay.

We cannot always detect true goodness on sight and we would be wise not to choose for ourselves but submit to Him who knows what is best for us. It is the shepherd not the sheep who leads to the right pasture. No child should be allowed to be governed by its own fancies, but by the father's love and discretion. It is the physician, not the sick patient, who decides what is needed.

Repeatedly in the Bible it says, the 'Lord is good' (Ps. 100: 5 and 106: 1, etc.). Jesus amplified this statement when He spoke to the rich ruler in Luke 18: 19, 'None is good, save one, that is, God.' Frequently we are told that the Lord will give 'good things to the upright', (see Proverbs 28: 10 and Luke 1: 53). Good things, then, can only come from One who is essentially good. The sad thing is that so many neglect the only source that can give us complete satisfaction. Many have grasped after things that appeared to be good, only to find that they were transient, synthetic and counterfeit.

What we must keep in mind is that this 'good thing' is not only related to things that are are temporal but includes our spiritual and eternal benefit. We must not judge the 'goodness' of God to us by observing only a part of our life; we must study the whole. There was a time, no doubt, when Joseph felt that God had forsaken him as he lay in the prison, but this was the testing time. When he reviewed his whole life he was able to say to his brethren as he considered his past suffering and ill treatment, 'God meant it unto *good,* to bring to pass, as it is this day, to save much people alive' (Gen. 50: 20).

Our main concern should always be to keep firmly walking the pathway of righteousness. Uprightness will inevitably receive its due reward both in time and in eternity.

26 Real Freedom

Then said Jesus to those Jews which
believed on him. If ye continue in my word,
then are ye my disciples indeed; and ye shall
know the truth, and the truth shall make
you free. John 8: 31 and 32

'Freedom' – this is a word that is on the lips of millions of people today. We constantly hear it echoing throughout the world. There is a charm and power attached to it that finds a response in every heart; it appeals to the sympathies that are universal and profound.

In recent years we have repeatedly witnessed the jubilant celebrations of those who have been granted political emancipation. No less than twenty-six free nations in Africa alone have emerged. Yet, paradoxically, at a time when man is struggling desperately to completely free himself, never have so many human beings been held in the grip of a power that they cannot control.

In this passage we have a wonderful promise of freedom given by Jesus, and it is vitally important that we pay attention to what He said in relation to this subject, if we desire to experience what He offers.

Notice the background to Christ's statement. The Jews claimed to be free politically, but in reality they were slaves of Rome. They claimed religious freedom but they were, in fact, in bondage to the letter. But Jesus saw that men could never enjoy perfect freedom because they were held captive by their own inordinate desires, resulting in moral, mental and spiritual darkness. They needed to be delivered from the thraldom of sin.

The Master Teacher said, 'Whosoever committeth sin is the servant of sin (V. 33). The reference here is of a man who is living a life of sin, that is, he makes this his constant practice, having no control over his desires. He is a prisoner in terrible bondage.

But what power or force can release a man from the chains of vice? Political and intellectual freedom do not give full satisfaction. They are incapable of liberating the whole man. Someone has said that political freedom is the bark, intellectual freedom but the fibre of the tree; spiritual freedom is the sap. Men contend for the bark and fibre. Christ gives the sap.

Verse 36 says, 'If the son therefore shall make you free, ye shall be free indeed.' The word 'indeed' occurs only here in the gospel of John and Westcott says, 'It appears to express reality in essence from within.' Here we come to the root of the matter. Real freedom is like the kingdom of God, it is within. This occurs when the citadel of the soul is controlled by the Prince of Peace. Because of this, nothing without can affect it. Joseph was just as free in the prison as he was on the throne.

Paul, although he was bound by chains, was free when he appeared before Agrippa, yet the king on his throne was a slave. Paul's statement was a classic example of those who know the true liberty of the sons of God. He did not say, 'I wish I was like you, O, king,' but he did say, in effect, 'I wish you could be like me! ' (see Acts 26: 29). Paul, the liberated prisoner, did not wish to change places with the enslaved king!

Notice the order of this promise. CONTINUE, KNOWLEDGE, then FREEDOM. Here are the steps to liberation. We must sit at the Master's feet in daily learning and living to grasp the truth. It is as we do this we discover that truth is not just a system, but also a power. Truth is not merely something we speak or write, it is much more; it is to be lived and felt. Jesus is saying here that truth and holiness are co-relative. To know truth is to know Christ in intimate fellowship and when we know Christ we will understand fully the words of Paul to the Galatians, 'Stand fast therefore in the liberty wherewith Christ hath made us free' (Gal. 5: 1).

27 A Sure Harvest

*Cast thy bread upon the waters: for thou
shalt find it after many days.*
Ecclesiastes 11: 1

The quotation of this verse sounds strange to western ears and the understanding of it is impossible unless we are acquainted with eastern customs. This, of course, is true with a great deal of scripture. Even so, there is a difference of opinion as to the true meaning of this passage.

The most popular view, which certainly accords with the context, is that the casting of bread or bread corn on the waters is referring to the custom of sowing seed by casting it from boats into the overflowing waters of the river Nile in Egypt. When the waters receded, the grain in the alluvial soil sprang up. Verse six certainly supports this view, which speaks distinctly of planting seed. Ellicott puts it like this. 'Cast thy seed even though thou canst not see where it will fall.' Yet there would inevitably be a good harvest.

The meaning then is that the people of God are to sow the seed of kindly deeds in faith and love, and although it may appear that our efforts are wasted, yet we are assured we shall reap a reward in terms of people finding peace with God. Jesus clearly endorses this promise in His classic Sermon on the Mount, where He speaks of the necessity of 'good works' as a means of leading others into the fold that they also may 'glorify your Father which is in Heaven' (Matt. 5: 16). What an encouragement this is to the Christian workers whose 'labours of love' have been constant over many years.

Many others have to encourage themselves in the Lord

as David did. We often have to say like the hymn-writer, 'Though often my toil seems but labour in vain, I leave with the Lord my endeavour!' and be sure that He will let nothing be lost that is done in His name and for His glory. Remember, 'Weeping may endure for a night, but joy cometh in the morning.'

The application of this figure is surely not restricted to acts of beneficence, but should also include the sowing of the Gospel seed by tract, youth work, Sunday school class, and the like.

Christian workers should heed the words of Dr. Campbell Morgan who said on one occasion, 'A child may forget what you have said in thirty minutes, but he will remember it in thirty years.'

It is our business to sow seed and God will give the 'increase'. He knows the right time and place to bring the seed to fruition. We must not jump to the conclusion that nothing has been accomplished just because we see no visible results. The work may have already begun which will manifest itself later on.

Recently, a bright young man came to the church where I am the minister. He was on his way to the south of England for a second term in Bible-college training for the ministry. He said, 'You do not know me, but I felt I had to call in to see you and tell you that I was converted in a campaign that you held about six years ago!' I remembered the campaign, but had no knowledge of his conversion. How very encouraging this news was 'after many days'.

Christian friend and worker, keep pressing on 'always abounding in the work of the Lord' (1 Cor. 15: 58). The great things of the Church are not accomplished by men who love the fanfare of trumpets and sensationalism but by the steady faithfulness of many unknown Christians who prayerfully stick to the task allotted to them. They shall in no wise lose their reward.

28 Resurrection Life

Jesus said unto her, I am the resurrection, and the life: he that believeth in me, though he were dead, yet shall he live. John 11: 25

The resurrection is the corner stone of the Christian faith. Without it the superstructure would crumble. If Christ was not raised from the dead said Paul, then we are 'of all men most miserable' (1 Cor. 15: 19). The resurrection of Christ makes the Christian religion different from all others. It is unique. Other religious leaders are dead. We have a living head. The symbols of the Gospel are not only a manger and a cross, but an empty tomb!

The ministry of Jesus demonstrated beyond doubt that He was the Lord of life. Four times He was confronted by death: the maid, Jairus' daughter, Mark 5: 41; the young man, Luke 7: 14; Lazarus, John 11.43; and, last of all, at the crucifixion.

Some, no doubt, would try to explain away the incident of the maid, saying she was in a coma. Regarding the young man on the bier, critics dismiss this by saying that there is evidence that some people have been buried alive, therefore this young man might have been. Lazarus is a more difficult proposition. Concerning the Saviour Himself, argument has been going on for 2,000 years, with all kinds of fanciful theories put forward in an attempt to undermine the teaching that Christ rose on the third day.

But the New Testament emphasises the fact of the bodily ascension of Jesus and in the last book of the Bible the doctrine is sealed with a testimony from the Lord Himself, who appeared to John in a vision saying, 'I am he that liveth, and was dead; and, behold, I am alive for evermore' (Rev. 1: 18).

The age-old question of Job, 'If a man die, shall he live

again?' is answered emphatically by Christ. 'He that believeth in me, though he were dead, yet shall he live.'

Yet Christ goes on to seemingly contradict Himself when He says in the next verse, 'whosoever liveth and believeth in me shall never die.' In one breath He says if a man dies and believes in Him he shall live; and in the next breath He says that whosoever lives and believes in Him shall never die. But there is no disparity here. Jesus is stating that all who are believers and die a temporary physical death will hereafter receive resurrection life. Then He goes on to state that the same prospects are for those who are alive and have faith in Christ. They 'shall never die', or, literally, 'shall by no means die for ever'. It was this blessed hope that enabled Paul to exclaim triumphantly 'For to me to live is Christ, and to die is gain' (Phil. 1: 21).

Notice the authority with which these words are spoken, 'I AM' not 'I will be'. We can know this living Christ NOW and share His lifegiving power, 'I live; yet not I, but Christ liveth in me' (Gal. 2: 20) should be the experience of all believers. The hope for eternity is received in time.

This is an experience that is vouchsafed to the 'whosoever'. Spurgeon's comment on this text is 'To the reception of Christ there is no limit however wrong, weak, unfeeling, hopeless.' Wise men are those who live in the light of eternity. 'Prepare to meet they God' is a message that applies to all, for all will survive this life, but the order and quality of life hereafter depends on what our relationship with Christ is now.

The Bible makes it quite clear that there will be a difference, 'And many of them that sleep in the dust of the earth shall awake, some to everlasting life, and some to shame and everlasting contempt' (Dan. 12: 2). It is to the believer's death alone that the glorious words apply, 'Blessed are the dead which die in the Lord' (Rev. 14: 13).

29 How to Know God

Be still, and know that I am God.
Psalm 46: 10

One of the outstanding claims of the Christian religion is that man can get to know God in a very real sense. Many, no doubt, would call this an arrogant assumption. Nevertheless, it is a fact and, as all committed Christians will tell you, it is a glorious and humbling experience.

In his Epistle, John wrote triumphantly, 'We know that we are of God' (1 John 5: 19). 'Know' is one of the key words of his letter, mentioned more than a dozen times. Paul also emphatically declares, 'For I know whom I have believed' (2 Tim. 1: 12) or, as Phillips puts it, 'For I know the one in whom I have placed my confidence.'

This is what happens at conversion; a personal encounter with God, an introduction, so to speak. Later on, Paul reveals his innermost desire – the craving of his heart; he writes to the Philippians (3: 10) and says, 'All I care for is to know Christ' (NEB). That is to know Him intimately, just as a child grows up to know his parents.

Here in this promise we are told how to obtain this knowledge. It is not associated with service, but with the sanctuary. It doesn't come from effort, but from repose. The trouble with most of us is that we can only talk about God in general terms. We speak only of the obvious; the things that are on the surface; few of us know anything about the deep things of God for the very simple reason that we are far too busy to find out.

There is a profound knowledge of God that can only be acquired away from the roar and rush, rattle and tumult of modern life. We get caught up in the round of committee meetings, conferences, rallies. We propound our theories and pass our resolutions. We spend time answering questions that have not been asked and failing to put forward questions that should be asked. We seem to be content with our carnal reasoning that has led us to a blind alley of frustration.

Furthermore, we seem not to realise why we have arrived at an impasse. Our ears have become deaf to the voice of the Holy Spirit when He emphasises that the answer to our dilemma is 'BE STILL'. We grope around like drunken men in the dark trying to find the way.

When are we going to learn that knowledge is connected with silence? To master a book, a subject, or a science, we have to be in the quiet place. The successful scientist spends long periods in his laboratory. The philosopher gets his inspiration alone in his study. To be successful and know the mind of God the man of God, likewise, must be found often in the secret place listening for the still small voice.

It is significant that all great men were prepared in the school of silence. Moses spent forty years in the loneliness of the desert. Ezekiel knew what it was to be in isolation on the banks of the River Chebar. David was alone with God three times a day. Paul went into solitary confinement for three years.

These were men of perception. They knew where they were going. They received a message from God for their generation because they were prepared to pay the price. The question is, are we willing to get alone with God?

If there is one promise above all others that this generation of Christians should grasp with both hands it is, 'Be still, and know that I am God.'

30　Needs Supplied

*But my God shall supply all your need
according to his riches in glory by Christ
Jesus.* Philippians 4: 19

The story is told that Queen Elizebeth the First asked a
rich English merchant to go on a mission for the crown
but he remonstrated saying that such a long absence would
be fatal to his business. The Queen replied, 'You take care
of my business and I will take care of yours.' The merchant went on his errand and when he returned he found
that his business, through the patronage and care of the
Queen, had increased in volume and he was richer than
when he left.

This is what Paul, in fact, meant when writing to the
Philippian believers about their supporting the work of
the ministry. They would not lose anything by putting the
cause of Christ first, indeed they would gain much. It is in
this relationship we must interpret the promise mentioned
here. Verse 18 says, 'Your generosity is like a lovely fra-
grance, a sacrifice that pleases the very heart of God'
(Phillips). Then the apostle goes on to affirm that God
would look after their affairs and that He had their in-
terests at heart.

God will be no man's debtor. He will repay a thousand-
fold. 'Give,' says Jesus, 'and it shall be given unto you;
good measure, pressed down, and shaken together, and
running over' (Luke 6: 38). This is the divine guarantee of
Christ.

This does not mean, of course, that all Christians have
to do to receive temporal and physical enrichment is to
pour money into the work of God. There is much more
to it than that. We are not to approach the kingdom of

God like a stockbroker looking for the quickest and best return for investments. We are to give without any thought of reward. We should gladly surrender all to the One who has done so much for us. This philosophy is so opposite to wordly reasoning and present-day trends. Carnal minds cannot understand such statements as 'There is that scattereth, and yet increaseth' (Pro. 11:24).

But the wonderful thing about giving to the cause of Christ is that physical as well as temporal blessings are often associated with it when the heart is right and all ulterior motives have been removed.

In the book of Malachi, God's people were given a definite promise that if they would only bring all the tithes into the storehouse the windows of heaven would be opened to them, they would have so much blessing that there would be no room to receive it and, 'I will rebuke the devourer for your sakes, and he shall not destroy the fruits of your ground; neither shall your vine cast her fruit before the time in the field, saith the Lord of hosts' (Mal. 3:11).

Many of us, no doubt, have been guilty of glibly quoting this promise, 'My God shall supply all your need', and have been disappointed because we failed to measure up to the teaching that is related to it. I wonder how many churches are impoverished because of the meanness and lack of sacrificial giving of time, talent and treasures? Oftentimes we deserve the rebuke that the prophet Haggai gave, 'Is it time for you, O ye, to dwell in your cieled houses, and this house lie waste?' (Hag. 1:4). We need to be continually reminded of the words of Christ, 'Seek ye first the kingdom of God; and all these things shall be added unto you' (Matt. 6:33). Here we have one of the keys to blessing in the Church. It is one of the secrets of revival progress.

Notice the source from which the needs of His people are met. Paul says, 'According to His riches in glory', or, as one translation puts it, 'Out of the greatness of His wealth.' Our God is well able to care for us and the wonderful thing is that when we put Him first in our lives our needs are often met without asking, the promise mentioned in Proverbs 11: 25 is made good, 'The liberal soul shall be made fat: and he that watereth shall be watered also himself.'

31   A Present Help

*God is our refuge and strength, a very
present help in trouble.* Psalm 46: 1

What a comfort this Psalm has been to the children of
God in all ages. Persecuted Christians in Europe, the
Quakers and the Scottish Covenanters derived encouragement and strength from its promises and triumphant declarations. It is said that Luther, when in trouble, was
accustomed to saying to his friend, Melanchthon, 'Come,
Philip, let us sing the 46th Psalm.' Then his face would
'brighten like the sky after a summer shower'.

We do not know for sure who the author of this Psalm
was, but it is generally agreed that the occasion was the
deliverance of Jerusalem from the army of the mighty
Sennacherib. That night when it seemed that all was lost,
God came to the aid of His people. He was their 'refuge'
and 'strength' and 'help'. It was a momentous deliverance.
Even the profligate Byron, infidel, yet true poet, burst
forth into lofty strains as he told how, 'The Assyrian came
down like a wolf on the fold'.

If there is one thing above anything else this verse tells
us it is that God is never more near to us than when we are
subjected to the pressures of life. This world is a beautiful
place, but it has its dark and gloomy side. Life has its ups
and downs. I receive many letters from people in distress,
heartbroken and lonely. Many of them are shut off from
their friends and relatives. What consolation is there for
them? Here it is in this promise. He is a 'present help',
which literally means, 'proved by experience'. Millions of
true believers would testify to the validity of God's faithfulness along this line.

78

Some time ago I visited a godly man who, because of his sickness and circumstances, had to spend many hours each day on his own. Each time I visited him he was always rejoicing and on this occasion he said, 'Oh, Pastor, the Lord is wonderful. I feel His presence always. He never leaves me alone!' How wonderful to know we all can have a companionship like that.

Some of us need to heed the advice John Wesley once gave to his friend who had said, 'I don't know what I shall do with all this worry and trouble.' At that moment Wesley noticed a cow looking over a stone wall. 'Do you know why that cow is looking over that wall?' queried the preacher. 'No,' replied his anxious friend. 'I will tell you,' said Wesley. 'Because she cannot see through it.' Then he said to his companion, 'That is what you must do with your wall of trouble – look over and above it to God who is our help.'

What we require is a childlike faith to believe that He is with us. 'My presence shall go with thee' is a promise to all believers. We do not have to strain and struggle, or whip ourselves into a frenzy like the prophets of Baal when they called upon their god for aid. We must learn to rest on God's word and leave Him to work things out for us. 'The Lord is at hand', said Paul when he was in prison. This was his constant comfort all through his ministry, even at the time of his trial when no man came to his support but 'Notwithstanding the Lord stood with me, and strengthened me,' affirmed Paul (2 Tim. 4: 17).

We should rejoice because the Lord is nigh to help. When we are toiling in His service, weary and discouraged, He is there to give grace, 'handfuls of purpose' and the increase to our labours. He is near to strengthen us when we are tempted and go through trials and troublesome times and it seems as though the mountains shake and the earth be moved. There may be an earthquake, but there need not be heartquake. In all these things we may triumphantly proclaim, like the Psalmist, 'Therefore will not we fear' because 'The Lord of hosts is with us; the God of Jacob is our refuge.'

32　The Peacemakers

*Blessed are the peacemakers: for they shall
be called the children of God.* Matthew 5: 9

There surely has never been a time when peacemakers
were more needed than in this age of wars and rumours of
wars. There is confusion and strife within the Church as
well as without. How we need this blessing of peace. It is
the preserver of life, prosperity and happiness.

Jesus, in His Sermon on the Mount, made a very significant statement in relation to this very important subject.
The designation 'children of God' is not applied primar-
ily to holy men of sterling character and full of good
works, although it must certainly include them. But the
chief role of His true followers, proclaimed the Great
Teacher, is that of a 'peacemaker'. That is a most interesting statement.

The Master implied that all who claimed to have His
disposition would be noted for their endeavours to bring
about a peaceful settlement of opposing parties. Harmony
and not discord would be their aim. They would always
strive to prevent contention. How many long, drawn-out
quarrels might have been averted if some kindly approach
by a third party had been made in the first place. It is possible, through a little tact and love, to help folk without
getting involved in argument. As the wise Solomon says,
'A word spoken in due season, how good is it' (Pro.
15: 23).

We must be careful, of course, to avoid intruding into
that which is quite clearly none of our business. We are
warned in the Scriptures against becoming a 'busybody
in other men's matters' (1 Pet. 4: 15). In some cases it
makes for a happier relationship by saying nothing.

Furthermore, we must not jump to the conclusion that only the 'children of God' work for peace. Many who have no Christian persuasion engage in activities promoting peace, but from entirely different motives and aims. We should also be on guard in our efforts to promote peace with others that we do not endanger ourselves. We must not make peace with men by breaking peace with our conscience. Real peace can only be brought about when it is based on truth or, as someone puts it, 'We must so seek the flower of peace as not to lose the pearl of truth.'

To carry out the work that Christ had in mind it is important for us to realise that we must possess a peaceable nature and we can only have this as we are reconciled with the 'God of peace' (Heb. 13: 20), and as we let His peace 'rule' in our hearts (Col. 3: 15). The Bible makes it clear how this may take place; we may have 'Peace with God through our Lord Jesus Christ' (Rom. 5: 1). It is, then, the peace 'receivers' who are in a position to be peace 'diffusers' and, as Faussett points out, 'God is thus seen reflected in them; and by the family likeness these peacemakers are recognised as the children of God.'

Now we should always keep before us the real work of peacemaking. We overlook the most essential part if we confine our endeavours to the settling of differences among men. Our first task is to attempt to get men to be at peace with God. When this happens they are likely to live in harmony with one another. This is one of the reasons why we are called to spread the Good News. It has the answer to our problems. It produces cordiality and goodwill, for the very Word we are exhorted to proclaim is called the 'Gospel of peace' (Eph. 6: 15).

The promise is that we shall be 'blessed' or 'blissfully happy' if we do this work. Our joy will know no bounds. Many Christians wonder why they do not experience the joy of salvation; they never seem to have that buoyancy of spirit. One of the reasons is that they look inwardly too long, instead of upward for strength and outward for service. The peacemakers whom Christ had in mind are God's happy children!

33   Promise to a Nation

Blessed is the nation whose God is the Lord.
Psalm 33: 12

The man who said, 'The nation that loses faith in God and man loses not only its most priceless jewel, but its most unifying and conserving force,' stated a solemn fact that is attested by history and present-day happenings.

In our own nation we have witnessed for several decades a drift away from God, resulting in a gradual lowering of moral standards we at one time cherished. The inevitable has happened; a permissive society has been born. The trend is to 'let every man do that which is right in his own eyes.' Almost every day we witness the evidence of such folly in a disregard of authority and violation of law and order. We have sown the wind, now we are reaping the whirlwind.

It might be argued by some that God's benediction can only rest upon the 'family of God', but the Bible teaches otherwise. God will always acknowledge and reward those who revere His name and respect His laws. 'Them that honour me I will honour' (1 Sam. 2: 30) is a principle that has been seen over and over again. Daniel made this clear when he enlightened the heathen king Belshazzar, 'O thou king, the most high God gave Nebuchadnezzar thy father a kingdom, and majesty, and glory, and honour' (Dan. 5: 18).

We are exhorted to pray, 'For kings, and for all that are in authority' (1 Tim. 2: 2). This would hardly be appropriate if they were excluded from receiving blessing from His hand. There is, of course, a vast difference in the kind of blessing from the 'spiritual blessings that are in Christ Jesus' bestowed upon the members of the Church of God.

Some may point out that history furnishes us with evidence that a nation can become distinguished without directly acknowledging the God of the Bible as did Egypt, Persia, Assyria, Rome and others. It is interesting to note, however, that a careful study will reveal that their religions contained principles that are clearly laid down in Holy Writ and that, in the practice of them, great prosperity resulted and remained with them until they departed from these principles.

In Egypt, they had a high moral standard. The spirit of benevolence prevailed. When an Egyptian died, enquiry was made as to how he spent his life so that due respect should be given to his memory. In Persia, a falsehood was considered in the most horrible taste and a liar was looked upon as the meanest and most disgraceful man. She educated her children so wisely that they were taught virtue as other children were taught letters. Rome, in her best days, exerted all her energy for the general good. The motto was 'no citizen of Rome must in any way wrong his brother citizen.'

Is there any wonder that these nations became great? When they practised these principles of righteousness they prospered. When they departed from them there followed the inevitable degeneration and lost glory.

We need to bring God back into the Church, the home and the heart. There should first of all be a humbling and confessing of our sins. Time is running out. Here is a promise to a nation. Who will heed it?

A few years ago General Montgomery appeared on television. He was reviewing the last war. He gave his version of it and what should be done in the future. He emphasised the enormous problems facing the world. Then he said, 'I want to finish this programme with a quotation from the Bible. Here it is in Deuteronomy 30: 19. 'I call

85

heaven and earth to record this day against you, that I have set before you life and death, blessing and cursing: therefore choose life! ' This is a message for our time and one to which we all should give due attention.

34 God's Goodness

O taste and see that the Lord is good.
Psalm 34: 8

How wonderfully different is the Bible from all other
books in its style and language. Many statements appear
to be contradictory and hard to understand, such as 'having nothing, and yet possessing all things' (2 Cor. 6: 10),
and 'when I am weak, then am I strong' (2 Cor. 12: 10).
They are, in fact, significant paradoxes with a profound
spiritual meaning. Some might raise an objection to this
phrase 'taste and see' on the grounds that before we are
likely to taste anything we would want to see it. This at
first sight would appear to be a valid argument until we
understand what it is all about.

The idea this promise conveys to us is that the things of
God cannot be known merely by observation. 'Seeing'
cannot satisfy the soul any more than a hungry boy would
be satisfied by looking at a shop with an abundant supply
of rich food.

In the spiritual realm, before we can see clearly and understand fully about the things of God, we have to have
an experience with God. The invitation here then is to experiment.

It is interesting that the word 'taste' is used. The language is drawn from the sphere of the senses and taste is
probably the simplest and safest of all the five senses. Our
eyes and ears, as with the others, may deceive us, but sel-
dom our taste. The thought then is that we may have an
experiment with God which shall be conclusive.

It is true to say that Christianity is glorious and blessed.
It is not merely a doctrine, it is something alive which
sweetens the whole of life. As the Scripture declares, 'For

he satisfieth the longing soul, and filleth the hungry soul with goodness' (Ps. 107: 9).

Notice the wonderful testimonies given in Psalm 34 concerning God's goodness. One cries out in verse 4 after being haunted by many fears, 'I sought the Lord, and he heard me, and delivered me from all my fears.' Then we have a group of godly folk who had known sorrow and of whom it was said, 'They looked unto Him, and were lightened' (V. 5) or as some translations have it, 'radiant'. Another confesses in verse 6 that he had been in many a difficult spot, but testified, 'This poor man cried, and the Lord heard him, and saved him out of all his troubles'. Then there is a most passionate pleading to others to come and put their trust in God.

The sad thing is that many fail to realise that there is such a thing as experimental Christianity. Many have full knowledge of the theory of religion, but no experience of the power. They know all about the mechanics, but nothing of the dynamics of the Gospel. They have a 'form of godliness' only. This accounts for the perpetual contradiction between creed and conduct.

Only when a man has found God in the sense that is mentioned in this verse is he safe from the subtleties of men. He will not then be 'carried about with every wind of doctrine' (Eph. 4: 14) or false prophets. He will be able to speak what he knows and testify of the things he has seen.

'Taste and see' is a simple, sound and effective way of testing the reality of God and His benevolence. Argument will not do it, for it is often subtle and unsafe. Even testimony can be unreliable and mistaken. But none of us will distrust the evidence of our own spiritual senses. We are assured that the 'goodness of God endureth continually' (Ps. 52: 1) and the wonderful thing is that all are invited to enjoy it!

35 Affliction and Glory

*For our light affliction, which is but for a
moment, worketh for us a far more
exceeding and eternal weight of glory.*
2 Corinthians 4: 17

Much of the so-called gospel preaching today is danger-
ously one-sided. There is an over-emphasis on the joy and
peace that will be received if one 'accepts Christ' as Saviour and Lord. While it is undoubtedly true that one is
benefited in every way by becoming a Christian, in all
honesty we should present the complete facts of the 'Good
News' to the unbeliever so that he will know exactly what
is expected of him if or when he turns to God in repentance. He will certainly experience 'life with a capital
"L"' but he should be told that he may also expect
trouble with a capital 'T' in following the Saviour.

We must never make it easy for people to come to
Christ. We deceive them if we preach a 'Come to Jesus
and all your troubles will be over' message. This sentimental, sugary, pseudo-gospel produces spurious converts
who inevitably suffer from spiritual maladjustment. It is
only as we declare the 'whole counsel of God' that we can
hope to build a strong Church.

Jesus made it perfectly plain to all who would become
His disciples that they must take up the cross. He was
candid with them and stated that it would mean hardship,
suffering, loss of friends, and so on. The highway of God
is difficult, dangerous and often dark. Paul and Barnabas
made this clear to the converts of the early Church in
Acts 14: 22 where their work is described as 'Confirming
the souls of the disciples, and exhorting them to continue
in the faith, and that we must through MUCH TRIBULATION
enter into the kingdom of God.'

But even if the pathway is hazardous; so long as it is the right way and God's way, this is all that matters. This in itself is the great consolation. To know that one is on the road that leads to safety and our eternal home is compensation enough for the hardships endured on the way.

Paul, in this text under consideration looks at this 'suffering' in its true perspective. Notice how he refers to his trials of many years. He refers to it as 'our light affliction which is but for a moment'. Paul's afflictions consisted of hunger, stoning, weariness, exposure to death on land and sea. He was constantly buffeted. Yet he used an expression as emphatically as possible to show that they were but a 'light affliction' in comparison to the benefits received. What is more, they appeared to him as if they were endured but for a moment of time.

The Apostle assessed the situation perfectly. It was not only the knowledge of being on the right path that gave him joy but also the amazing reward awaiting him at the end of the journey – an 'eternal weight of glory'. Moffatt's translation of this promise is, 'The slight trouble of the passing hour results in a solid glory past all comparison', or, as Goodspeed puts it, 'is piling up for me an eternal blessedness.'

Nothing happens by chance to the child of God. Even our troubles, Paul said, 'worketh for us'. Here is the striking promise. We often see the benefits of adversity even in this life, and through it we are driven to God, we are purified, and our understanding of the ways of God becomes clearer.

Christian pilgrim, compare your sufferings with what they are actually producing for and in you, then you will come to the same conclusion as Paul, who regarded his afflictions as mere trifles. They are transient, short, even in the longest life. But the reward has no limit to its duration. It is, literally, everlasting. And remember, 'If we suffer, we shall also reign with Him' (2 Tim. 2: 12).

36   The Door

I am the door: by me if any man enter in,
he shall be saved, and shall go in and out,
and find pasture. John 10:9

For a full and happy life three things are needed. God, who knows man's basic requirements, has made such a provision and these are promised by Christ to all who are admitted into the Church, the entrance to which can only be through Christ Himself. 'I am the door' is the emphatic declaration.

This is vitally important for all to grasp when seeking God's plan for their lives. The Church does not have the prerogative of her Leader. Ceremonies, professions or achievements cannot bring man into a state of grace. The message of the Gospel is clear, 'Neither is there salvation in any other' (Acts 4:12).

But none need despair about entering, all may approach and 'any man' is welcome. This is the most liberal invitation imaginable. The figure employed here, depicting Christ as a door, shows only one aspect of the Lord's life and signifies His condescension and concern for men. Because of its simplicity, even the most prosaic minds would be able to understand and appreciate.

There is here described a fairly comprehensive picture of the state of those who are 'in Christ'. Notice, then, the threefold promise given. Firstly, the believer is SECURE: 'He shall be saved.' This is a great Bible word and it covers the whole area of man's life. The Scriptures make it plain that salvation means He has saved us, He does save us and He will ultimately save us. It deals with our past, present and future.

Here in this particular passage it deals mainly with our

present state. The pardoned sinner, pursued by the memories of his dark and evil deeds that are like a pack of wolves, is safe in the fold. The door is shut against them. He is secure from all alarms.

Then we are given another picture of the believer, he is FREE. 'And shall go in and out.' We used to sing years ago, 'I am free, free, free. Christ has made me free. Once I was blind but now I can see; I am free, free, free.' But to some, Christianity seems to mean adopting a set of negative rules. They would bring folk into bondage instead of the glorious liberty of the sons of God. They fail to see that the Gospel is not condemnation but emancipation.

Furthermore, this description 'GO IN', access, is contrasted with 'AND OUT', egress, which surely makes for Church progress. On the one side we have the interior union with Christ and on the other there is reference to the exterior where we are active for Christ. Some never go 'OUT' into the 'highways and byways'. They are engaged in no service to help their fellow men. Some never go 'IN' to enjoy sweet communion with the Lord. Real freedom is related to both.

The third promise here is that the child of God will be NOURISHED. He shall 'find pasture'. In Christ all the needs of humanity are met and satisfied. He makes provision for the whole man to be nourished, intellectually, emotionally, and spiritually. He sustains by His love, power and presence. Wherever He leads, we are assured that when the need arises and we become spiritually hungry and thirsty, we shall be able to say like David, 'He maketh me to lie down in green pastures: he leadeth me beside the still waters.' What more could we ask for in life?

Every committed Christian will agree with the testimony of Harry Dixon Lees who wrote, 'All that I need is in Jesus. He satisfies, joy He supplies; Life would be worthless without Him. All things in Jesus I find.'

37 He Cares

Casting all your care upon him; for he careth for you. 1 Peter 5: 7

Recently I heard a lady missionary give a very interesting talk. She spoke about the doubts and fears that rob us of the peace we all need so much in a world of turmoil and strife. She gave a very dramatic illustration out of her own experience to prove her point.

One day her husband had not arrived back at the mission station at the appointed time from one of his trips into the bush. She became apprehensive when nightfall arrived and he had still not returned. Her suspense gave way to sickening worry when suddenly she heard the sound of tom-toms in the distance. She wondered if this was the signal for trouble.

The missionary retired behind closed doors to pray. After a while she heard the noise of the drums coming nearer and nearer, right up to the mission station, in fact. The din was frightening. Then suddenly all went quiet for a few moments, followed by muffled conversation. Then came hurried footsteps across the verandah to the door. The missionary by this time was in a cold sweat, with her heart beating wildly, and wondering what would happen next. The door opened quickly and there stood her husband! He had been detained by the natives who wanted to escort him back and to bring gifts to celebrate their anniversary, which she had forgotten!

In the circumstances we might forgive the missionary for being somewhat disturbed, although she was quick to confess the futility of harbouring such distressing thoughts and cares that lead to sheer panic.

It is these needless, subtle and soul demoralising 'cares'

that are referred to here in this promise. It does not refer so much to burdens as anxieties – unless we mean the burden of anxiety. But it means much more than that. We are invited to commit the whole of our cause to Him. The amplified version brings this thought out very clearly. We are exhorted to cast 'the whole of your care – all your anxieties, all your worries, all your concerns, once and for all – on Him.'

Most of us are so easily subjected to nagging doubts. We become gripped by despair, thinking about what might happen. Often we are unduly anxious about the welfare of our children, we get over-concerned about our job, health, future, until we almost anticipate things going wrong. These are the things that will crush the spiritual life out of us if we try to go it alone. Worry robs us of the joy of salvation. It also affects us physically. The medical authorities tell us that 'worry kills more people each year than cancer or heart disease.' The cares of this life can be a terrible scourge.

Here we are offered relief and consolation. The Divine Companion is near, waiting to help. He who is concerned about the falling sparrow and is attentive to the young ravens when they cry will not forget us. 'Are ye not much better than they?' asked Jesus of His disciples.

'For He careth for you' is the comforting promise. He knows, He loves, He cares. Then let Him take control. He alone can deal with the past, the present and the future. He not only waits to help, but He longs to do so for we are more dear to God than we can ever imagine. Phillips makes this explicit when he translates this verse as, 'You can throw the whole weight of your anxieties upon Him, for you are his personal concern.' That's good enough for me and I hope it is for you!

38 The Church Triumphant

I will build my church; and the gates of hell
shall not prevail against it. Matthew 16: 18

At a time when the Church is being assailed by evil
forces without and 'godless' men within the ranks of
Christendom are advocating the disintegration of the
Christian Society as it is at present constituted, these
words of Jesus come to us with fresh force. They inspire
confidence. At a glance, we realise there is no need for
alarm regarding the permanence of His cause.

His sovereign plan cannot be thwarted. This 'building
of God' will forever stand majestically secure. The might
of men and devils cannot destroy the divinely erected citadel. 'The gates of hell shall not prevail against it,' said
the Master or, as one translator puts it, 'the powers of
the underworld shall never overthrow it.'

It is most interesting to study the circumstances when
the Son of God made this decree. It is an amazing predic-
tion as well as a promise given to His followers. He made
the profound statement, 'I will build my Church' to a
group of weak disciples at a time when, naturally speaking, there was not the slightest hope of success; the com-
munity of believers to which He referred was as yet only
in the embryonic stage; His own ministry, to all outward
appearances, was a failure and to crown it all He informed
them that He would soon be put to death as a common
malefactor!

Can we find in all history a comparable prophecy to
this? What makes it the more remarkable is the actual
fulfilment of it. The building process has gone on right up
until this present twentieth century. It has had universal
influence and has embraced people of all nations. This

fact alone should be enough to convince the most hardened unbeliever of the divinity of Jesus Christ.

Christ's Church is distinguished from all other forms of organised societies by its peculiar origin and growth. No other organisation has ever been constituted as this one. It stands unique in the annals of history. The simple reason why the Christian Church stands supreme is because its founder was One who died and rose again from the dead.

It is significant, also, that Jesus did not tell His disciples to go and build the Church. He informed them that this was His responsibility. He was to be the founder and the foundation, the architect and the builder. The teaching of the New Testament stresses this constantly. It also points out that the Lord accomplishes His work through the co-operation of men of His choice (see 1 Cor. 12: 28, Eph. 2: 20 and 4: 12). Paul, for instance, who was a faithful co-labourer, is described in 1 Cor. 3: 10 as a 'skillful architect and master builder' (Amplified) but he is quick to add in the next verse, 'For other foundations can no man lay than that is laid, which is Jesus Christ.'

It is of the utmost importance then that we heed the words of the Apostle to the Corinthians, 'Examine yourselves, whether ye be in the faith.' We pride ourselves on being members of a Catholic Church, a Church of England, a Baptist Church, a Pentecostal Church, etc. What we should be really concerned about, however, is whether we are members of His Church. One thing is certain, that is, 'the Lord knoweth them that are His.'

The Church of Jesus Christ is not a material building. It is no particular visible church made of brick or stone or marble. It is made up of all true believers of every name and rank and race.

The word 'church' literally means 'called out' and is applied to God's spiritual children; called out of the world into the fellowship of His Son. All other man-made institutions and organisations will pass away, but His church will continue to be a testimony to God's power and grace. It will go on growing until the last member is in. It will continue its function in the ages of eternity. I hope you are in it. If not, read John 1: 12 and 10: 9. There we are shown quite clearly the way to become a member of the only Church that really matters.

39 The Way to Happiness

*Blessed are they which do hunger and
thirst after righteousness: for they shall
be filled.* Matthew 5: 6

I believe it was George Bernard Shaw who said on one
occasion that he did not want to be happy, he had no time
for such luxury! However, the majority of people on this
planet, it is safe to assume, desire to live a contented and
happy life. It certainly makes for a better relationship to
have a good genial neighbour or workmate than a good
miserable one.

This subject is not a superficial or unimportant one. A
world that is filled with people who are radiantly cheerful
is a safe world. Happiness is a basic requisite for the security of the home and the nation.

The Great Teacher of 2,000 years ago realised more
than anyone else that all men born into the world need
their quota of joy. A man without a song is a dreary fellow indeed. It is not the will of God that we should spend
our life in the slough of despond with our spirits constantly dejected. He has planned something better for us.

Most of us make the mistake of trying to brighten up
our lives by seeking abundant life as a prize. We try to ac-
quire it through pleasure, wealth, social functions, fame
and the like, but most of these give only transient thrills.
They are poor substitutes for the satisfaction we all need.
The truth is, that happiness comes to us as a by-product
of an unselfish life.

Jesus preached a sermon on the subject that is recognised as a 'classic'. It has seven main points to it. Here we
are concerned with one aspect that is vitally important. If
we act upon its instruction we will experience the inner

'fulness of joy' of which the Bible speaks.

To obtain it Christ said we must 'hunger and thirst after righteousness.' Nothing could express the ardent desire of the soul better than hunger and thirst. It is not enough to applaud righteousness, we must crave for it like a starving man. We must long for it like one in a desert desperately seeking water.

Someone has said that 'the lack of appetite for righteousness is the curse of mankind.' Certainly there is ample evidence to hand to show that many are surrendering sound moral principles for monetary gain, quick promotion or some such selfish gratification. They ignore the fact that the road of self-deception inevitably leads to dissatisfaction. If we chase a mirage we must not be surprised if we end up filling our mouths with sand.

It is interesting to note that the NEB substitutes for the word 'righteousness' the words 'to see right prevail', and C. B. Williams states 'Being and doing right'. We must do right and at the same time be men of integrity. Our lives must correspond with our actions. We must reject the pharisaical attitude of 'Don't do what I do, but do what I tell you.'

We are not even to seek righteousness for the reward it brings, but for the glory of God and the benefit of others. Here lies the secret to the whole matter. Self must be completely eliminated. It is when we yearn to obey God in this respect that we will experience the soul rapture which so many great men of God have written about. We shall 'be filled' is the promise, or, as Weymouth puts it, 'completely satisfied.' In the light of the clear instruction that we have here regarding a full and complete life, how appropriate are the words 'If you know these things, happy are ye if ye do them' (John 13: 17).

40 Lifted Up

Humble yourselves therefore under the mighty hand of God, that he may exalt you in due time. 1 Peter 5: 6

One of the chief characteristics of the true children of God is humility. They emulate their Master, of whom it is said, 'And being found in fashion as a man, he humbled himself, and became obedient unto death, even the death of the cross' (Phil. 2: 8). There we can trace the seven steps of humiliation that the Saviour took, followed by the seven steps of exaltation, commencing in verse 9 with the statement, 'Wherefore God also hath highly exalted him.'

Here the pattern is set for all Christians who desire to please God and be effective in His kingdom. It is made perfectly clear in the Scriptures that God hates pride in any form. The Bible states that he 'resisteth the proud' but he 'giveth grace to the humble', or, to use a more modern translation, he 'elevates' them.

Note the significant admonition here, 'humble yourselves'. It is our personal responsibility to keep a constant watch on our lives lest we think more highly of ourselves than we ought. We must never harbour an exalted estimation of ourselves but always keep low at the Master's feet. We have nothing to boast of but the grace of God. What we are and what we have is all of His mercy.

The Apostle Paul gives a solemn warning in Gal. 6: 3, 'If a man think himself to be something, when he is nothing, he deceiveth himself.' When we begin to entertain a high opinion of ourselves then the germs of spiritual decay begin their deadly work and we thwart the purpose of God for our lives.

We do well to follow the advice in 1 Pet. 5:5, which says, 'Be clothed with humility.' Here, this virtue is likened to a cloak and our spiritual security is sure when we wrap ourselves in this garment. We should see to it that we put it on daily.

To get a clearer understanding as to what is involved to bring us into the place where we may enjoy the blessing of this promise, it is also necessary for us to consider the context where we are exhorted to 'submit yourselves one to another' (Eph. 5:21). Christ did not ask the disciples to wash His feet, but He did tell them to wash one another's feet. God is greatly concerned about the relationship and harmony of His children. Humility is the key to the state of peace in the Church. Our practice should always be 'in honour preferring one another' (Rom. 12:10).

Now notice the awesome phrase, 'under the mighty hand of God'. Whether it is for chastisement, discipline or protection, we are to bow before Him and yield to His will. He knows what is best for us. At times it is difficult to understand what He is doing, but we can be assured that His mighty hand is controlled by the mighty heart of love.

When we resign ourselves to His will, then we can expect that in 'due time' deliverance will come or, as it says here, 'That he may exalt you'. One translation states, 'At the right time He may set you on high.' God did this for Joseph and David and others. The way of yieldableness is certainly the way of fruitfulness. In His own time He will reward the faithful with good things from His bountiful hand. This will not only be a time of rejoicing but character strengthening as well. The thought here surely includes vindication when He will set on high the ignored and despised children of God.

This was the thrilling testimony of Hannah, that great saint of God in the Old Testament. After she had been misunderstood and suffered anguish of soul, she experienced this divine uplifting and graphically exclaimed in her prayer in 1 Samuel 2: 7-8, 'The Lord maketh poor, and maketh rich: he bringeth low, and lifteth up. He raiseth up the poor out of the dust, and lifteth up the beggar from the dunghill, to set them among princes. . . .' This is the heritage of all God's trusting children.

41 Deliverance from Fear

The fear of man bringeth a snare: but
whoso putteth his trust in the Lord shall be
safe. Proverbs 29: 25

Fear can be a blessing as well as a curse. It can be the
means of preserving us from some terrible calamity. A
healthy respect for the tremendous power of the flame
will enable us to take the necessary precautions to keep
it in check. Fear is an excellent servant but a terrible
master. We should continually be on guard against its influence. There are many kinds of fears that bring torment
to the soul, not the least of these is the fear of man.

It is surprising how many of the great men in the Bible
were gripped by this sinister thing. Some of the chief
rulers who believed in Christ did not confess him because
they were afraid of the Pharisees. Peter (Gal. 2: 12) did
not eat with the Gentiles because he feared the Jews.
Elijah was so scared, not of a man but of a woman, that
he ran three days journey into the wilderness!

Even the great king, David, a man after God's own
heart, succumbed to this evil force when chased by Saul.
1 Samuel 27: 1 states: 'And David said in his heart, I shall
now perish one day by the hand of Saul: there is nothing
better for me than that I should speedily escape into the
land of the Philistines.' This mighty warrior knew what it
meant to be snared by fear. It almost robbed him of the
throne for which he was anointed king.

I wonder how many Christians throughout the Church
are held in its paralysing clutches? Fear is robbing the
Church of youth workers, Sunday-school teachers, sick
visitors, open-air preachers. Because of the fear of man
we fail to protest against the moral and social evils of our

time. Why is it that the Church is not on the march like an army terrible with banners, proclaiming the Gospel of Christ in its fulness? In many instances it is not because we have no message; it is because of the fear of what man will say or do or think of us, and so false cults, the humanists and politically-minded, have a field day whilst the Church lies haunted and terrorised in a dungeon of despair, shackled by this demon of fright.

We need to be reminded of the message of Paul to Timothy, 'For God hath not given us the spirit of fear; but of power, and of love, and of a sound mind' (2 Tim. 1: 7). The promise to us all is 'Whoso putteth his trust in the Lord shall be safe.' As we learn to put our confidence in Him, to rely on His strength, then we are more than a match for the opposition.

David had to take himself in hand to overcome this terrible malady that cripples even the strongest of hearts. He looked away to God. When he did that he got a new vision of the Almightiness of God and he was reassured. He was able to say in Psalm 56: 3, 'What time I am afraid, I will trust in thee.' It is interesting to note that he goes on to state, 'I will not fear what flesh can do unto me' and then he expresses his confidence that he will overcome all opposition and writes, 'this I know; for God is for me' and at the end of this psalm he again exultingly emphasises the point by exclaiming, 'In God have I put my trust: I will not be afraid what man can do unto me.'

When we look around we can be so easily alarmed and it is not much better when we look within. We have to confess that we do not have the power to deal with the situation, but when we look above we have hope, we see an open heaven with spiritual resources available to cope with any eventuality. When we let the Lord of those resources take over our lives, we will exclaim, like Paul in Philippians 4: 13 (Phillips) 'I am ready for anything through the strength of the one who lives within me.'

42 The Eternal Word

But the word of the Lord endureth for ever.
And this is the word which by the gospel is
preached unto you. 1 Peter 1:25

The story is told that in the last persecution by the pagans against the Christians there was in the service of the Emperor an apostate Christian. During the discussion as to how best to crush the Christians, the deserter said, 'It is of no use to burn the Christians, for if you burn every Christian alive today, and leave a single copy of the Scriptures remaining, the Christian Church will spring up again tomorrow.' Such was the power of the Word of God. The Emperor thought he could banish it and issued a decree ordering the destruction of the Scriptures but, like many others, he found this to be an impossible task.

The Christian Bible is an indestructible volume! History attests it. Right from the start of the gospel age it has flourished in the midst of adversity. When Herod had done his utmost to stem the advance of the Church, he was removed from the earthly scene and the record states, 'But the word of God grew and multiplied' (Acts 12:24). It has always been the case. Time and again attempts have been made to get rid of the Word of God, but it has proved to have an enduring quality. It has eternal power in it!

It cannot be destroyed because this Word is the supreme abiding revelation of the will of God. It is a living organism, not a haphazard collection of fragments. It breathes life because it contains life imparted by the Holy Spirit. This is the Word that we have received into our hearts. As 1 Peter 1:23 declares, 'Being born again, not of corruptible seed, but of incorruptible, by the word of

105

God, which liveth and abideth for ever.'

What we must always remember about the Bible is that it doesn't merely *contain* the Word of God, it *is* the Word of God and when men submit to it and accept it they are transformed into the sons of God. As Peter adds significantly, 'And this is the word which by the Gospel is preached unto you.'

What wonderful consolation is here for God's children. His cheering promises, His assurances that there is a brighter, better world, remain permanent. Amidst all the revolutions on earth, the changing scenes, patterns of thought, the fading glories of all that is material, His truth stands forever the same. Kingdoms rise and fall, but His Word is as firm as a rock. Man rises to power and fearful heights and then he becomes enfeebled. The darkness of death comes down upon the mighty men of the world as inevitably as the night settles on the earth, but the Living Word shines on like a beacon. It never loses its vitality. It remains just as beautiful with the passing of time. There is no fading of its glory. The gospel sound is just as musical as ever. It has as much authority now to save as it had when it was first applied to the human scene. Time has, in fact, enhanced the message.

We are here assured, then, of its never failing comfort. It has proved to all unbiased men that it is what it claims to be, the very Word of God. It lives because He lives! Men still rebel against it, but sooner or later it vindicates itself. Judgment inevitably follows its rejection and eternal blessing is consequent upon its acceptance. We do well to remind ourselves that God's truth and moral laws have been fixed for all time. As the Psalmist has declared, 'For ever, O Lord, thy word is settled in heaven' (Ps. 119: 89). The choice is left with man either to accept it or reject it.

43 The Dead in Christ

*And I heard a voice from heaven saying
unto me, Write, Blessed are the dead which
die in the Lord from henceforth: Yea,
saith the Spirit, that they may rest from
their labours; and their works do follow
them.* Revelation 14: 13

Note carefully the words of this promise. It is not
'blessed are the living' but 'blessed are the dead'! Here in
this portion of the Bible we see a shaft of light penetrat-
ing the gloomy vale of tears. Celestial music with its
cheering notes bursts forth to silence the sobs of broken
hearts who can find no comfort because their loved ones
are no longer with them. Amidst the awful storm and the
terrible thunder of the Devil's mocking voice spelling out
abject despair, comes the news from above to give assurance that death is not a blind alley; it is not the end but
the beginning of a more glorious existence than hitherto!

Did you know that Christians are never more alive than
when pronounced dead? And did you know that the child
of God is better off dead than alive? This is not to say, of
course, that the followers of Jesus do not enjoy their stay
on this earth. Indeed they do. It is the most thrilling, ab-
sorbing and purposeful life possible. There is nothing dull
about the existence of a man who is fully committed to
Jesus Christ. His joy is 'unspeakable'. He experiences
'life more abundant'. Yet Heaven offers more. The blessings of the city of God surpass by far anything we may
experience here. The place itself has an indescribable
magnificence.

Writing about it, the Rev. John Bate relates, 'Let a man
take a survey as far, as wide, as deep and as minute as his

mind will enable him, of the beauties, the sublimities and the magnificence of all the works of God and of man as they lie out on the broad surface and in the great depths of the earth, and ask if such are the glories which compose and enshrine the footstool and the vestibule, what must the glories be which adorn and compose the palace – the abode of His throne. If the workmanship of the outer court is so superb, what must that be which is exhibited within Heaven itself?'

Here in this promise one corner of the veil separating time from eternity is lifted and we get a brief glimpse into Heaven. It should be sufficient to reassure us that our loved ones are in a far better place than we who remain. They are free from all weariness, pain and heartache. They 'rest from their labours'. The word 'labours' refers to harassing, exhausting, painful labours. It does not mean rest from work. Heaven is not a place of idleness. We will still have the capacity for the employment of our energies. But we will be occupied in a grander scheme than what we have known down here.

'Their works do follow them' is a striking thought. This is all that will follow a man into eternity. We cannot take gold, land, or any of the honours we might have received in this life. But character and the results of it will be evidence that a man belongs to Christ. God's people will realise that the pilgrim journey that may have been so hazardous and demanding was a part of the divine plan. That day we shall see that our labours have not been in vain in the Lord. What consolation is found here for all who are yielded to Christ. The day is fast approaching when the whole Church will be united as one. The heavenly family will be complete. 'Blessed are the dead which die in the Lord!'

44 First Things First

But seek ye first the kingdom of God, and
his righteousness; and all these things shall
be added unto you. Matthew 6: 33

I heard a man sometime ago say, 'I grab all I can get. If you don't look after yourself nobody else will.' He was evidently caught up in the rat race of 'every man for himself' attitude that is prevalent today. Now there is nothing wrong in trying to better oneself. All of us, no doubt, like to taste some of the luxuries and comforts of life.

But there is a danger in becoming so absorbed with the idea of 'getting on' that we lose sight of the Christian fundamental principles that will enable us to better our station in life and at the same time get the fullest satisfaction out of material things.

The teaching of Jesus on this subject is, as to be expected, profound, but will no doubt be puzzling to many people. He was a practical teacher. He was concerned about the physical needs of His followers. What they should eat and the clothes they should wear, and so on. Why should not Christians share some of the best things in life and occupy the most influential positions? It is folly to imagine that only the godless should be comfortably off and be highly successful in their vocations.

A great deal of good has been done for God by wealthy Christians who have been faithful stewards of that with which He has blessed them. However, whilst we may not all be prosperous, we can be assured that our needs will be met if we put into practice the formula of Christ.

Firstly He tells us that we should not fret over these matters. We may be concerned about our meagre fare but we should never be unduly anxious about it if our lives are right before God. In verse 31 of this same chapter the Master says, 'So don't worry and don't keep saying, "What shall we eat, what shall we drink or what shall we wear?"' (Phillips). Worry will make the situation worse.

Secondly, we should rest in the knowledge that God sees our predicament. Verse 32 says, 'your heavenly Father knoweth that ye have need of all these things.' Christ points out that the One who feeds the sparrows and clothes the flowers of the field will certainly look after His own children.

The third request is vitally important. 'Seek ye first the kingdom of God, and his righteousness.' In other words, put first things first. What a magnificent promise this is coupled with a blessed invitation. Christ came to build a kingdom, the character of which is righteousness, and He seeks to enlist workers to co-operate with Him in building it and to make it their main consideration in life. The guarantee is that if we make this our supreme pursuit all things needed for the present life will be added or, as one translation puts it, 'these things will come to you as a matter of course.'

There are traditional sayings ascribed to Jesus, one of which is believed to be authentic and is quoted by Origen and Clement of Alexandria. 'Ask great things and little things will be added to you: ask heavenly things and earthly things will be added to you.' Really, we should be more concerned with Heaven's bounties and if, as Paul says in Colossiahs 3: 1-2, we are 'risen with Christ', a term which means living in communion with Christ, then 'set your affection on things above, not on things on the earth.' In other words, keep your priorities right. The blessedness of the Christian experience depends on what is dominant or uppermost in our life. What we can say with certainty is that this formula of the Master Teacher has worked for two millenniums and thousands of dedicated Christians today would readily testify to its validity.

45 Blessed are the Meek

Blessed are the meek: for they shall inherit the earth. Matthew 5: 5

The story is told of a missionary who, when teaching a class of little black boys on the meaning of meekness, asked the question, 'Who are the meek?' A boy answered, 'Those who give soft answers to rough questions.'

This is certainly not far from the mark. Meekness, however, must not be mistaken for weakness. A person who possesses this quality is one who is disciplined and has learned to control himself. A meek man is a disciple constantly watching and praying, who has developed Christian character. He continually sits at the Saviour's feet, learning of Him who is 'meek and lowly in heart' and finding rest for his soul.

We are told there was no word in the Greek for meekness. The nearest is meanness. It was something inconceivable and unknown to them. If it was present in human life, they could not understand it; the man would be a puzzle and would be described by a misnomer.

In the present day we have the words meekness and humility, but they are still comparatively unknown by the world; in fact, a character full of meekness and gentleness would, according to the judgments of men, be a man without fire and spirit. Men of the world today, like the Greeks long ago, are confused. They see nothing of great significance in this noble Christian grace. To many, a meek man is a contemptible man who lacks manliness and authority. They cannot see the vast chasm between meekness and meanness.

But God has chosen this virtue to make a man noble and of sterling character! We see this in the case of

Moses, who was one of the greatest men of history. The Bible says about him, 'the man Moses was very meek,' above all the men which were upon the face of the earth (Num. 12: 3).

God can use such men of quiet disposition and humble soul. It is an essential qualification for true greatness.

The value of meekness is seen here in this promise, 'They shall inherit the earth.' What an astonishing statement and promise! This probably refers to the prophecy of Daniel 7: 27, but there is a wider, general and continuous fulfilment also. In this life it is the self-controlled, patient, mild man who is, in the long run, the most prospered and lives the most satisfying life. His serenity helps him to experience the maximum joy in all conditions of life, but a man who spends his time in disputes and is harassed, passionate and impulsive, cannot enjoy even what he possesses. There is constant war in his soul and as a result he is filled with fear and is lacking a sense of security.

Christianity, then, is not 'pie in the sky', it affects a man's life in every department, including the material side. Paul in writing to Timothy says, 'godliness is profitable unto all things, having promise of the life that now is, and of that which is to come' (1 Tim. 4: 8) or, as the NEB says, 'the benefits of religion are without limit.'

Scattered throughout the Bible there are a number of different promises given to the meek, such as 'The meek will he guide in judgment' (Ps. 25: 9), 'The Lord lifteth up the meek' (Ps. 147: 6), 'He will beautify the meek with salvation' (Ps. 149: 4), and many more. There is no doubt about it that God expects His children to possess this virtue. He has made provision for us all to develop our Christian character along this line, as Paul reminds us in Galatians 5: 23, that the fruit of the Spirit is meekness, thus enabling us not only to be recipients of blessing from God, but to be profitable servants for God.

112

46   Unjust Criticism

For with what judgment ye judge, ye shall
be judged: and with what measure ye mete,
it shall be measured to you again.
Matthew 7:2

Here is a promise with a difference and one that we are
apt to quickly pass over without realising its import and
how it vitally affects our relationship with our fellow men.
If we took more notice of such promises our churches
would be in a far happier position and the fellowship
much sweeter than it often is.

The text, so it is affirmed, was a proverb amongst the
Jewish people. Whether it was so or not, it certainly expresses a truth that Christ accepted as conveying His own
sentiments. It is, in fact, the rule by which God will deal
with His people. He will treat them as they treat others.

The RSV makes this promise a little more clear. 'For
with the judgment you pronounce you will be judged, and
the measure you give will be the measure you get.' There
is, then, a sense whereby we can choose for ourselves
whether God will be merciful or severe to us.

What we are warned about here is not the legitimate
constructive criticism done in the spirit of meekness with
the aim of restoration, but it refers to the harsh, preju-
diced, condemning criticism which is Pharisaical. We
should avoid it at all costs. Someone has likened a person
with a censorious spirit as one with a 'vulturous nature
which smelleth out carrion.' It is an evil thing indeed and
brings retribution.

This is a great principle in the divine administration.
The principle, of course, works both ways. If we measure
out to others kindness, consideration, love, then it will

113

return to us in the same measure; if severity, malignity and rigour, then we can expect these things to come back upon our own heads. The measure you give will be the measure you get.

The story is told that a little boy went home to his mother one day and complained to her saying, 'Mother, I went into the garden today and we were playing together and shouting about when a boy kept mocking us.' 'What do you mean, Johnny?', his mother queried. 'Well, I called out "Ho," and this boy said "Ho," then I said to him, "Who are you?" and he answered "Who are you?" Then I said, "What's your name?" and he answered "What's your name?" I replied, "Why don't you show yourself?" and he answered "Show yourself." I then went into the wood to look for him, but could not find him, so I shouted, "If you don't come, I will punch your head," and he said, "Punch your head." '

His mother then said to him, 'Ah, Johnny! If you said, "I love you," he would have said, "I love you." If you had said, "Your voice is sweet," he would have replied, "Your voice is sweet." Whatever you said to him, he would have said back to you,' and the mother then gave him the following advice. 'Now, Johnny, when you grow up to be a man, whatever you say to others, they will, by and by, say back to you,' and his mother pointed him to the text of Scripture, 'With what measure ye mete, it shall be measured to you again.' Let us beware lest we become malicious and our words return to us like some sinister, haunting echo or our deeds act as a boomerang to smite us.

The context points out what is very often the case today, that it is the fellow who has least right to point the finger at others who complains. It is worth noting that Jesus gives some sound advice to this man in Matthew 7: 5. A modern translation is, 'First go and pull the plank out of your own eye before trying to remove the splinter

114

from your brother's eye.' How we need to guard our hearts and keep a bridle on our lips. If we are ever called upon to pass any judgment upon others, let us always keep before us the advice of Paul when he wrote to the Galatians, 'Considering thyself, lest thou also be tempted.' There is great safety in having a magnanimous spirit.

47   No More Pain

*And God shall wipe away all tears from
their eyes; and there shall be no more death,
neither sorrow nor crying, neither shall
there be any more pain: for the former
things are passed away.* Revelation 21:4

Christ spoke as authoritatively of Heaven as He did
about other vital subjects. It is the homeland for God's
children. 'In my Father's house are many mansions,' said
Christ, 'I go to prepare a place for you' (John 14:2). It is
significant also that He said these words, 'If it were not so,
I would have told you.' If Heaven had been a delusion we
can be quite certain that Jesus Christ would have com-
mented on this, but our hope is well founded. It is no
shrewd guess or dream, it is a reality.

One of the wonderful promises about this heavenly
land is 'There shall be no more pain.' Heaven will be free
from tears and heartache. Suffering will have ceased for
ever. There will be no fevered brow to soothe, no waiting
beside deathbeds, no more agonising visits to hospitals
to look with pity upon the mentally retarded and incur-
able. How often have I seen the look of anguish on a
mother's face when she has sat by the bedside of a sick
child, frustrated by a feeling of helplessness and unable to
bring relief to the frail, fever-stricken body of one she so
dearly loved. Pain is universal. It strikes oftentimes without warning. It is impartial. Kings as well as peasants
come under its domination.

I have witnessed grown men weep in a paroxysm of
agony and no doctor has been able to subdue its power.
Most people have felt the excruciating stab of pain. Some
have had it as a constant companion. They seem to get no

relief from the awful scourge. They have to learn to live with it.

There is a pain that no medical treatment can overcome. Science can invent nothing to banish the pain of grief from the human heart. The agony that comes to loved ones whose partners have deceived them or have been unfaithful is not cured by a doctor's prescription. The jilted lover's anguish of soul is not easily mended. The heartache of a child whose parents have parted cannot be eased by money or a holiday. Pain has never been conquered by man.

We cannot understand why so much of what is good and necessary is associated with pain, like the birth of a child, for instance. The problem of pain is a very real one, but in Heaven for the first time we shall be really free. We shall be governed by a new order. The God of Love will be in control.

There is a land that has been specially prepared for the redeemed which will know no sorrow. Tears will be wiped away, gloom will give way to glory and despondency to rapturous delight. No institutions will be needed to deal with infirm, deranged and diseased people, for our bodies will be different. This corruption will have put on incorruption. He, whose sole aim is to 'steal, and to kill, and to destroy' will be forever banished. The sin question, which is the root cause of pain, will be dealt with. This indeed will be God's utopia. A land of indescribable glory and serenity, described by Isaac Watts in the words:

> There is a land of pure delight,
>   Where saints immortal reign;
> Infinite day excludes the night,
>   And pleasures banish pain.

48 The Waiting Guest

Behold, I stand at the door, and knock: if
any man hear my voice, and open the door,
I will come in to him, and will sup with
him, and he with me. Revelation 3:20

Is it possible to witness a more pathetic scene than this?
Here we see a fine church building; regular services are
held in it; there are the usual religious activities; the
members are influential, rich and well groomed; the
minister, we may safely assume, feels proud that he has
aspired to be in charge of such a fashionable congrega-
tion. Over the doorway of this beautiful edifice is the in-
scription: 'The Church of the Laodiceans' but, alas,
Christ is outside trying to gain admittance!

This church was situated in Asia Minor but serves as a
solemn warning to Christendom as a whole. Christianity
without Christ makes a mockery of New Testament
teaching. It is a contradiction of all that the Apostles
stood for. Today we have a similar situation in many
places. We need to put Christ back into the pulpit and the
pew, and to let Him take His rightful place in the heart
and in the home.

The words of this promise reach far beyond the limits
of the 'lukewarm' members of this Laodicean commun-
ity. The phrase 'any man' is wide enough to embrace
those who have sunk to the uttermost depths of deprav-
ity as well as those like the prodigal's self-righteous elder
brother. We can be assured that where there is a closed
heart there is always a knocking Christ.

What amazing condescension is manifested here. The
words of this text express the infinite patience and long-
suffering of Christ. Outside the bolted door of human
hearts He is standing, speaking, knocking. On the one
hand there is obdurate stubbornness and on the other

118

love and tenderness that pleads again and again for entrance.

The Saviour is not easily offended by our persistent denials of His offer of friendship. If we disregard Him, He does not disregard us. The call from His lips to those who spurn His love is always, 'If any man hear my voice, and open the door, I will come in to him.' Here is the wonderful gospel call and magnanimous invitation which is constantly going out to the sons of men.

The promise of the text is that Christ will give perfect satisfaction. 'I . . . will sup with him, and he with me.' This is a banquet of love and communion wherein is such joy and contentment that it beggars description. This cannot be experienced by theoretical analysis of the Gospel of Christ. It is not so much the message but the Master who meets our need and brings us into a new dimension of living.

Much depends on our giving attention to the words, if we 'hear' his voice and 'open' the door. We must open our hearts and invite the King of Glory to come in and take His rightful place. It requires decision and action on our part.

Campbell Morgan emphasised a man's responsibility along this line when he told the story about Holman Hunt's picture. He said that when Holman Hunt painted that wonderful picture of the thorn-crowned King outside the door, knocking, he showed his picture to his dearest friend in the study before it was publicly exhibited. His friend looked at the kingly figure of Christ, at the rough and ready door, and at the clinging tendrils which had spread themselves over the door. Suddenly he said, 'Hunt, you have made a terrible mistake here.' The artist asked, 'What mistake have I made?' and the reply was, 'Why, you have painted a door without a handle.' Hunt replied, 'That is not a mistake. The door has the handle on the inside.'

49   Praise the Lord!

*Whoso offereth praise glorifieth me: and to
him that ordereth his conversation
aright will I shew the salvation of God.*
Psalm 50: 23

There are two main thoughts in the fiftieth Psalm. We
have the picture of the righteous Judge and also the
righteousness that is required by Him. God makes a de-
mand on our lives and it is only as we obey His commands that we find satisfaction in life. The first thing we
should seek to do, is to get a correct relationship with God
and work in harmony with Him. Everything falls into
line when we do this.

Before there can be fulfilment of this promise we have
to give consideration to two requirements. One is PRAISE.
Thanksgiving should play a vital part in our Christian experience. We are quick at asking, but not so ready to
thank God for the benefits that He has bestowed upon
us. Too often we are self-centred and forgetful.

The Psalms are full of exhortations to praise the Lord,
but how often do we do it? A rejoicing heart is conducive
to spiritual growth. Offering praise to God is an act of
worship which should be our daily practice. Hardness of
heart, which hinders the flow of divine life, cannot exist
when we have a spirit of gratitude. Furthermore, true
thanksgiving also includes confessing our weaknesses as
well as acknowledging God's favour. That is why the Psal-
ter says, 'It is a good thing to give thanks unto the Lord.'

Notice the other requirement in relation to this promise, he 'ordereth his conversation aright'. This does not
refer to speech, but to something more important. The
word 'conversation' actually refers to a way of life. It
means to change our course of life, our attitude, and

walk the way of uprightness. It is not enough to praise the Lord, we are expected to walk with the Lord. We must honour Him with life and lip. When we do this we glorify God, and, as someone has said, this should be man's chief aim in life.

When a man glorifies God, he finds true fulfilment in his Christian experience. It is then that we will experience the full salvation of the Lord. God has many things to give His children, but many remain in spiritual poverty because their lives are not measuring up to the standard of the Word of God. It is folly to expect God to bestow His precious gifts upon us if we do not meet the conditions that He has laid down for the fulfilment of His promises to us.

This word 'salvation' embraces a very wide area. It speaks of the deliverance, safety and general blessings that come to us from the good hand of our God. It is related to our past, present and future. It affects our body, soul and spirit. It is God's provision for a fallen world and it comes to us not through a plan, but a man – the man Christ Jesus.

Here it is very significant that He will 'show' the salvation of the Lord to those who do these things. This promise is repeated throughout the Bible. He will manifest His power in the lives of those who will obey His Word. He will work out His purposes amongst them. To be able to give proof of God's presence amongst us is the need of the hour. Thank God it is gloriously possible to say to the sceptic, as Moses did to the troublesome Israelites, 'Stand still, and see the salvation of the Lord.' The world is tired of hearing about this Gospel; they wait to see a demonstration of its power. When we do our part, He will do for us as He did for the early disciples, 'confirm the Word with signs following' (Mark 16: 20). It is then that we are likely to hear the outsider saying, in the words of the Psalmist, 'Salvation belongeth unto the Lord' (Ps. 3: 8).

50 Comforted

*Blessed are they that mourn; for they shall
be comforted.* Matthew 5: 4

Jesus was not only a very great preacher, but one who
had great perception as well. He could see the need of
mankind and His words of wisdom were directed to meeting that need. Christ never spoke on irrelevant subjects.
What He said was always relevant to the situation at
hand. He never talked over the heads of people, but to the
hearts of His hearers. There was purpose in everything
He did. His aim always was to help people. How we need
to learn from the Master Teacher in our dealings with our
fellow men.

In this particular passage Jesus shows His concern
about those who 'mourn', the meaning of which goes far
beyond the thought of sadness as a result of loss of friends
or possessions, although it may include them. The reference is to those who have gazed long and hard at their
own failures and wickedness of their own heart and, as a
result, have humiliated themselves before the Almighty
and have confessed their unworthiness. They know what
it is to cry like David, 'I am a worm and no man' (Ps.
22: 6).

This feeling of being incapable of rising to achieve anything for God because of unworthiness seems to have
been the experience of many great men of God. Indeed
the more they sought God the more they saw the sinfulness of their own heart and the less confident they became of their own abilities.

And yet these are the very ones upon whom Jesus pro-
nounces a benediction! 'Blessed,' says Jesus, or how
happy, are people in such a position! Such sorrow of
heart leads to reconciliation with God. As Paul points out

in 2 Corinthians 7:10, RSV, 'For godly grief produces a repentance that leads to salvation.'

They are blessed because they have discovered the secret of true godliness. All pride has been banished, unworthiness has bowed before almightiness. Such condescension, confusion and brokenness will inevitably bring divine approval upon all who experience such abject despair for themselves.

'They shall be comforted,' says Jesus. They will find consolation in the knowledge that God is ever ready to forgive, cleanse and renew the soul. All those whose estimation of their own ability is nil, will experience the enveloping love of God. They will know assurance and peace.

This word 'comfort' is a very soothing, blessed word indeed. We can rejoice in the fact that our heavenly Father is called 'the God of all comfort' (2 Cor. 1:3). This is the very nature of God, benign, gracious and tender towards the lowly in spirit. Many will endorse the testimony of Isaiah when he said, 'And in that day thou shalt say, O Lord, I will praise thee: though thou wast angry with me, thine anger is turned away, and thou comforted me' (Is. 12:1).

Let all those who feel that they are too weak and insignificant to be of use in the work of God find cheer here that our God not only will restore the penitent soul but He will elevate such to be of service in His kingdom. In fact, these are the only people that God can really use.

This state of mourning is what we may call the blessedness of sanctified sorrow. It leads to effectiveness in the work of Christ and surely the greatest comfort that can possibly be experienced is to feel the hand of God upon us in blessing, enabling us to play a vital role in promoting His cause. This state of 'blessedness' that Jesus speaks about in this promise should be the desire of all true Christians.

51   Not Forgotten

For God is not unrighteous to forget your work and labour of love, which ye have showed toward his name. Hebrews 6: 10

This is a most encouraging promise for many faithful workers in the Lord's vineyard. It is to be regretted that very often years of constant and sacrificial labours have brought no word of thanks, no acknowledgments, but have in fact been taken for granted. This is a common fault in many churches. No genuine Christian works for the praise of men, yet a word of appreciation makes the task much more enjoyable and worthwhile.

How we ought to thank God for the many who have toiled behind the scenes, workers who have given years of unstinting service. Let us thank God for those who always cheerfully respond to a challenge. Whenever called upon they never complain, but come forward to meet some particular need. These are the great 'backroom workers', so to speak, who are helping to keep the Church of Christ going. They are not in the public eye, but nevertheless are doing a vital work and are making a great contribution to the progress of the Gospel.

One thing is certain, if man forgets, God does not. He 'is not unrighteous to forget'. God sees all that we do in secret or behind the scenes. He knows what is done and the motive behind the act. Nothing can be hidden from the eyes of Him with whom we have to do. He is not unjust, unmindful, or unfair.

He watches every act of kindness. He will honour every consecrated worker who has diligently carried out his menial tasks away from the public gaze. Whatever we do in the cause of His kingdom is remembered.

We do not serve an ungrateful Master. The inference here is that we shall be recompensed for services rendered! How amazing this is. It is sufficient reward to know that he shows interest in our work, apart from receiving acknowledgment for our efforts in His cause.

We should also note that God often prepares His great men in this way. He watches the reactions of those whose labours have been hard and constant, which have not been acclaimed by men. God knows that if we are faithful in that which is least, we are likely to be faithful in that which is great. If we work with no ulterior motive when we are away from the eyes of them, it is quite certain we will do so if we are projected before the public. That is why God brought Gideon from behind the oak, Moses from the desert place and David from the sheepfold. The 'reward' has often been promotion in status in His kingdom.

We must not be discouraged if we have been overlooked or ignored. The Master of the vineyard knows all things. The righteous Lord is in control. He will bring great satisfaction to us and glory to His name.

One thing we must always learn is that faithfulness is exceedingly important in the Christian life. We should, in fact, always be living in the light of eternity, having in mind what Christ will say to those who have constantly endeavoured to do His will. 'Well done, thou good and faithful servant.'

Let us keep plodding on, rejoicing in the great privilege of having some part to play in the great cause. Whether or not our work is noticed or acknowledged by men, we are assured that our God not only sees what we do but will suitably reward our services in this life and in that which is to come.

52 The End of the Road

Mark the perfect man, and behold the upright: for the end of that man is peace.
Psalm 37: 37

It is unwise to draw conclusions as to the faithfulness of God towards His people when a life is only half lived. There are, of course, certain things that happen in life that are difficult to understand; but He who knows the end from the beginning will make manifest His will in such matters in the eternal day and we will not be disappointed. The all-wise God knows what is best and we must trust Him at all times, even when we cannot understand what He is doing.

As we travel through life, God's purposes sometimes seem to be thwarted and hopes of a bright future fade as the storms of life break with terrifying fury and beat upon the timid pilgrim walking the pathway of righteousness. The Devil mocks as the crushing blows of adversity fall upon his head. The darkness can be overwhelming.

How easy it is on occasions to lose heart and cry, 'Hath God forgotten to be gracious? . . . Is his mercy clean gone for ever?' (Ps. 77). No doubt Joseph felt like that when he languished in the prison. No doubt the tempter whispered that he would have been better off had he succumbed to the desires of the temptress. Often it appears that lying, deceit and crime pay big dividends in terms of promotion and material gain. David points this out in verse 35 of this Psalm: 'I have seen the wicked in great power, and spreading himself like a green bay tree.'

But this, of course, is only part of the story. What is the final outcome of a life that is opposed to the moral and spiritual laws of a holy God? David goes on to describe the position of the 'wicked'. The flourishing of the godless, described here as a 'green bay tree', inevitably suffers from the moral decay that is inherent in their nature. Verse 36 says, 'Yet he passed away, and, lo, he was not. yea, I sought him, but he could not be found.' Frequently in this life, as well as in the next, men reap the harvest of a sinful life.

Notice the contrast at the 'end' of each life, of the godly and ungodly. 'The end of the wicked shall be cut off' (v. 38), and the reference to the upright man is 'the end of that man in peace.'

There are two helpful translations which throw light on this particular verse. The Amplified is, 'Mark the blameless man and behold the upright, for there is a happy end for the man of peace.' Rotherham says, 'Mark the blameless man and behold the upright, for there is a hereafter for the man of peace.' Here we have a twofold thought which is that God will ultimately bring the upright into a state of blessedness both here and hereafter.

The man who walks according to the rule of Scripture will have no regrets at the end of the earthly journey. He will review his life and will be satisfied with God's plan. He will also be able to look into eternity and rejoice in the glorious hope that is laid up for him in the city of God. It is as we surrender fully to God that we will be given the same assurance as the poet of the Old Testament had. 'Surely goodness and mercy shall follow me all the days of my life: and I will dwell in the house of the Lord for ever.'